MW00652254

Dedicated to all the wonderful people over the past century, who have contributed to making Corona del Mar the beautiful community that is truly "The Crown of the Sea."

Within the past decade, Steve Simon, local artist, has published five books on his paintings covering California, Hawaii, Laguna Beach, Newport Beach and Orange County. A prolific and talented artist, Steve has produced hundreds of paintings within that time frame. A Newport Beach resident, Steve has graciously created the cover illustration for this book, and other Centennial paintings which are on display in his Balboa gallery.

Image courtesy of the Corona del Mar Centennial Foundation

The History of
Corona del Mar
Centennial Issue

By
Douglas Westfall

The Paragon Agency
Publishers
2004

The History of
Corona del Mar
Centennial Issue

Douglas Westfall 1949—

Published by
The Paragon Agency
Orange, California
2004

1. Corona del Mar
2. California Seaside
3. California History
   I. Title
   II. Author

ISBN: 1-891030-49-3

Library of Congress Control Number:
2004097968

Printed in the USA
1k, r1

Title page photograph courtesy of Howard Folsom

THE CORONA DEL MAR CENTENNIAL FOUNDATION

Centennial Mission Statement

The mission of the Centennial Celebration is to bring together the entire community in celebration to honor the 100-year birthday of the village of Corona del Mar. Along with special event celebrations, history, education and community involvement, The Centennial Foundation launched a community fundraising campaign to support the events, The Centennial Plaza and Time Capsule to honor this special time in our history and inspire future generations for many years to come.

Executive Committee

Centennial Executive Director & Committee Chairperson: Peggy Fort
The Corona del Mar Centennial Foundation Chairperson: Bernie Svalstad
Ex-Officio City Representative: City Manager, Homer L. Bludau
Fundraising & Sponsorship Committee Co-Chairs: Peggy Fort & William Dean
Marketing & Publicity Committee Chair: Peggy Fort
Community Outreach Committee Chair: Beverly Johnson
History Committee Chair: Laura Dietz
School Involvement Chair: Jan Billings
Art Liaison Chair: Steve Simon
Special Event Committee Chair: Tim Brown
Gala Events Committee Co-Chairs: Wade Roberts & Toni Van Schultze

Centennial
Foundation
CORONA DEL MAR
1904–2004

ACKNOWLEDGMENTS

The Corona del Mar Centennial Foundation Board of Directors
Executive Director: Peggy Fort

Board of Directors Officers:
Bernie Svalstad, Chairman
Mark Schulein, Vice Chairman
Wade Roberts, Treasurer

Board Members:

Claudia Agudelo
William Dean
Luvena Hayton
Beverely Johnson
Linda Rasner
Jim Skahan

Jacqueline Wittmeyer
Ex-Officio:
George A. Berger
Tina Hoover
Scott Palmer
Ron Yeo

Contributing Editors:
Laura Dietz
Dr. William O. Hendricks
Helen Fairfield
Peggy Fort

A special thank you to The City of Newport Beach

Photo Credits:
Sherman Library & Gardens, The Newport Harbor Nautical
Museum, First American Title Corporation and Harbor Photo.
Cover illustration, courtesy Steve Simon.

The Corona del Mar Centennial Foundation
The Corona del Mar Centennial Foundation is a not-for profit,
tax-exempt 501 (c) (3) association committed to investing in the
Corona del Mar community through celebration of the history,
education, art, and physical community enhancements for
present and future generations to enjoy, while preserving the
historic significance of the village. Federal Tax ID 200330457

CONTENTS

PREFACE

From age five, I remember coming to the beach each summer. We came first to the tidepools when we were little, then as we got older, we went to the state beach where the waves were a little more gentile than at the local pier. Invariably we always came to Corona del Mar.

I remember finding my first crab, crawling among the rocks; and sliding down the bluffs, long before it was considered dangerous. I learned to swim with the waves at Corona del Mar State Beach, and to surf at 23rd street in Balboa.

As a historical writer and publisher, I've produced books on American history, special events, and cities — large and small. Now with the release of *The History of Corona del Mar,* I seem to have come full circle.

I wish to express my thanks to the people of this community for the privilege of producing this book.

Douglas Westfall
Publisher

FOREWORD

The year 2004 marks the 100th anniversary of the founding of Corona del Mar. Although it has been part of the city of Newport Beach for the past 80 years, Corona del Mar has always been, and remains today, a distinctive portion of the city, set somewhat apart. For instance, unlike other parts of the city, its address is specifically Corona del Mar, not Newport Beach, and it has its own zip code, not part of the Newport Beach zip-code series.

Perhaps this is also why, even though Newport Beach can boast a fairly sizable number of books dealing with its history, very little in any of those books deals with Corona del Mar's history. In fact, except for a series of articles appearing in the Sherman Library & Gardens newsletter almost 25 years ago, virtually nothing has been written on the history of Corona del Mar itself. That is, until now, with the publication of this book.

I have been pleased to work with Doug Westfall in helping to put together this book, which is being published by the Corona del Mar Centennial Committee. I hope the community finds it of interest and enjoyable.

William O. Hendricks
Director, Sherman Library

CHAPTER 1
Rancho by the Sea

The land surrounding Corona del Mar was once a vast rancho that stretched *from the mountains, to the sea...* Actually, it ranged from about Red Hill in north Orange County, to the harbor — but not the peninsula. Still the 48,800 acre rancho encompassed everything from Newport Bay to Laguna, and reached well north of the Santa Ana freeway. Most of the land in the northern portion was a swamp, known as *Ci´naga de las Ranas* or the swamp of the frogs. Rather an inglorious name for what we now call Tustin.

A panorama of Rocky Point.

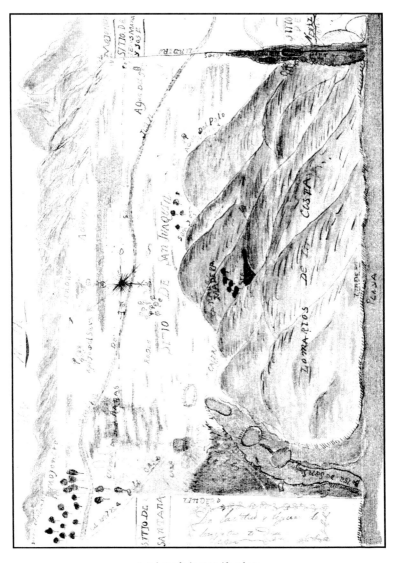

Jos´ Andr´s Sep´lveda's
Dise˜o of Rancho San Joaqu´n.
Courtesy California State Archives

The frogs were so numerous that people could travel at night from San Juan Capistrano to Los Angeles, and follow their sound that could be heard from miles away. In spring and summer, the water level was so high, that a road had to be taken up in the foothills just to get by. Today that trail in Tustin is appropriately called Foothill Road.

Jos´ Andr´s Sep´lveda petitioned for a rancho in 1836. He was the *Regidor* (Prefect) of Los Angeles, whose father had been a *Soldada de cuera* (Leather Jacket) at the Mission San Gabriel. He did not receive his land grant until the following year however as there was unrest in California, and there were five governors during that year alone. (One even governed twice.)

The following year, *Juan Jos´ Alvarado* was in office as Governor, and was in support of the idea of ranchos. Sep´lveda then received his rancho in 1837, but only the mountains and the swamp, not the sea. He and his wife *Mar´a Francisca de Paula Avila Sep´lveda* had 12 children and lived somewhat northwest of the upper bay of Newport, near what is now Santa Ana.

The Yorba and Peralta families held the adjacent rancho, the *Santiago de Santa Ana,* since 1810. They were both descendant from Juan Pablo Grijalva, who founded the great rancho (78,000 acres) in 1801. In 1841 however, the Yorba family and then the Mission San Juan Capistrano, both complained that Sep´lveda's grant encroached upon their land rights. Sep´lveda then petitioned for a second land grant, the *Rancho Bolsa de San Joaqu´n:* the land reaching to the sea. This, he was to quickly receive the following year, as Governor Alvarado was still in office.

Saint Joachim was Mary's father and bolsa in Spanish, means pocket. Not pockets of water, but pockets of land as is seen today in the upper bay, where the marshlands reach up above the water. Bolsa de San Joaqu´n was named for those pockets of land. The boundaries of the old rancho was moved, satisfying the Yorbas and the Mission was secularized, ending that issue. Sep´lveda combined the remaining rancho land of the northern half, with the new lands of the south, to create the new rancho of almost 50,000 acres.

Mexican California did not last long, just five more years and in 1847, the Mexican American War forced the California government to capitulate to the Americans. Now California was part of the United States — to be granted statehood in just three years. Gold was discovered in Northern California in 1848, and the rush of Americans and others the following year, raised

NATIVE CALIFORNIANS THROWING THE LASSO.

Vaqueros on the ranch.

the population of California from 5,000 to 50,000 in just 12 months. Southern California however, languished as people flooded the north, leaving the south alone.

Sep´lveda had built a large house and the good times of the period allowed him to enjoy a rich life. Cattle was king and thousands of animals, roamed over the lands. Sep´lveda was rich for the times. Called *El Rico,* he favored fine clothes, great fiestas, and a popular diversion of the day: horse racing.

There was at the time, a grand horse brought from

Sep´lveda astride Black Swan.
Courtesy of the Bowers Museum

Australia: *Black Swan.* Large and powerful, Sep´lveda knew he had to race this horse. He arranged to race the animal with his close friend Teodoro Yorba, against Pio Pico's famed horse Sarco.

Pio and his brother Andr´s both wagered on Sarco as Sep´lveda and Yorba did on Black Swan. Pio had been the last Governor of Mexican California; as Andr´s had been General of the Californio Army.

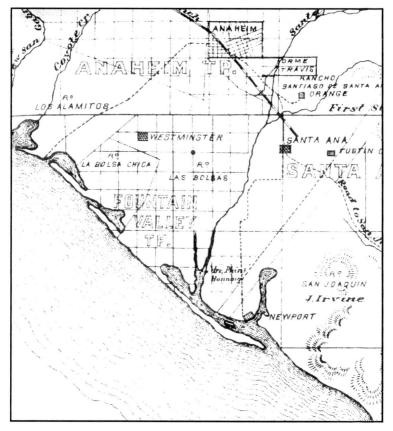

Early map of the north Orange County coastline, 1880.

A bet valued at $50,000 (in money, cattle, horses, and land,) came in 1852 and Black Swan won by 75 yards. Such high wagers were common, the loser thinking nothing of it, as a new wager would come along. Sep´lveda acquired Black Swan and is shown in the painting by Henri Joseph Penelon.

Pio Pico borrowed $15,000 from one Don Able Stearns, an American who had become a Mexican citizen in the 1830s. Stearns foreclosed on Pico, adding his rancho to his own holdings.

In 1854 a Land Commission was formed to confirm the some 800 land grants that dotted the California landscape. Sep´lveda had his title proven, but not until a dozen years later. Just over 600 land grants were ever confirmed.

The beginning of the 1860s seemed prosperous for the southern California rancheros. Cattle ranged free on the lands, rainfall came to 20 inches a year, and the American government had brought peace to the countryside after a quarter of a century of Mexican government upheaval. This however, was about to change.

Pio Pico

A disastrous flood came in 1861. Farmlands were ruined however, most operations in southern California were ranches, not farms, and they were running cattle. In 1862 however, came the start of what was to be a three year drought. This drastically hurt the finances of the rancheros and took most of the cattle in the region. Horses were shot, to save fodder for the remaining cows — as cows had more value than horses.

So many dead animals filled the range, that huge piles of dead carcasses were set afire. Near the shore lines, dead animals were pushed over the bluffs, to be washed out to sea. Northward in Rancho Palos Verdes, such an ocean strand was named the bone yard, for the many cattle bones that showed up over the years.

Rocky Point, south of McFadden Landing.
Courtesy of the Sherman Library

Sep´lveda's situation was no different than most, and he began to borrow money at exorbitant rates: six to eight percent per month. Just $500, borrowed at 5% a month, brought a debt of $5,500 after only five years. That same $500 at 8%, would rise in the same time, to over $60,000.

Sep´lveda borrowed to maintain his lifestyle: first $15,000, then $10,000 more, then another $6,000, then $5000. The last loans paid off the first, but as foreclosure loomed in late 1964, he sold his beloved rancho for $18,000. Don Jos´ Andr´s Sep´lveda died a decade later in Sonora, Mexico.

By 1866 the rains returned, but this time with a vengeance, for they created the greatest flood in California history. The dry lands were washed to the sea and small towns suffered greatly from the down pour. Newly formed Anaheim had most of its buildings damaged and the adobe structures destroyed.

One *zanja* (watering ditch) of a rancho, became a torrent and changed forever the course of the San Gabriel river. It now flows far east of its original river bank and washed much of the surrounding lands, into the ocean.

Because of the drought and floods during the mid-1860s, only sheep could be raised on the southern California countryside. The cattle were mostly dead and so many of the horses had been shot. The ranchos were decimated, and soon most of the rancho owners were gone.

"The place was barren, no people, no cultivation..."
Quote from a visitor to Southern California

By this time, the largest landholder in southern California was Able Stearns. He had amassed some 200,000 acres of prime land through unscrupulous means. Following the Civil War, sheep ranchers in the north, also took advantage of the situation in southern California.

The Flint-Bixby company up north near

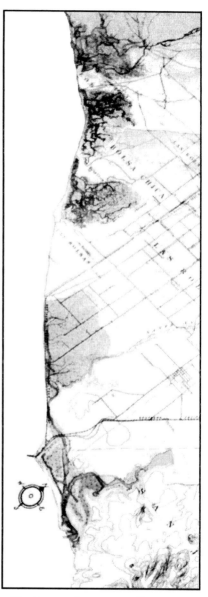

The Orange County coastline, 1894
Courtesy of Costa Mesa Historical Society

Monterey, owned the Rancho San Justo, a 54,0000 acre rancho. Moving south, they later obtained the Rancho Los Cerritos for $20,000. Llwellyn Bixby, and cousins Dr. Thomas and Benjamin Flint had formed the company for the purpose of sheep ranching and had originally driven 20,000 head of sheep from Iowa to California. Sheep wool was becoming valuable as the American Civil War, had halted the production of cotton.

Here in the south, they acquired Rancho Los Palos Verdes and Rancho Cajon de Santa Ana. Jotham Bixby and John Bixby too, came south to work the ranchos and acquired Rancho Los Alamitos from Stearns. Together, they held some 100,000 acres in control. As the second largest landholders in all of southern California, they were only beginning.

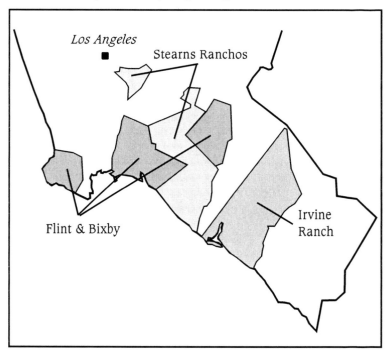

Sheep ranches in southern California.

CHAPTER 2
The Ranch of the Irvines

Born in Belfast of 1827, James Irvine was the 8th of 9 children. Immigrating to the United States in 1846 he worked in New York at a paper mill until hearing of the gold rush in California during 1849.

Taking passage to Central America, he crossed Panama and obtained transport on a Dutch ship. During the more than 100 days of travel, he met Collis P. Huntington and Benjamin Flint, two men who would someday, greatly change the landscape of California.

A panorama of the bay, from the cliffs.

James Irvine (1827-1886)
Courtesy of The Irvine Museum

During the gold rush, James Irvine had tried the gold fields, but soon went to San Francisco, became a grocer, & sold vegetables and dry goods. Forming *Irvine and Company,* James invested his profits in real estate. At the highly inflated rates of the day, he garnered some wealth. James I married in 1866, to Henrietta Marie Rice; James II was born the following year.

Going into partnership with Flint-Bixby, Irvine helped establish and own half of, what was to become the Irvine Ranch. Acquiring the *Rancho San Joaquin* in 1864 for $18,000 (48,803 acres,) *Rancho Lomas de Santiago* in 1866 for $7000 (47,227 acres,) and a strip of Rancho Santiago de Santa Ana by 1868 (12,157 acres.)

A dozen years later, Irvine bought out his partners interest for $150,000. This became the Irvine Ranch: one-fifth of what

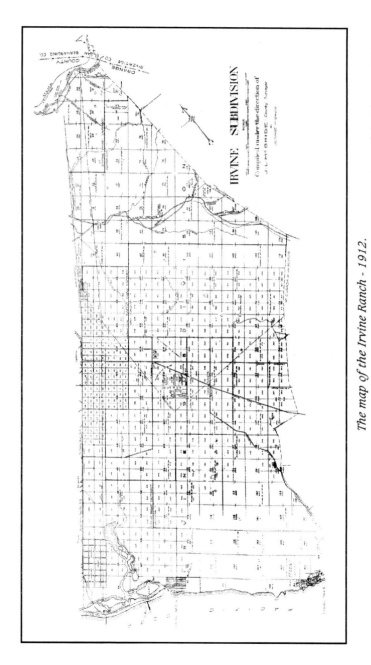

The map of the Irvine Ranch - 1912.

Courtesy of the Sherman Library

Rough waters of Rocky Point..

Courtesy of the Sherman Library

would become Orange County; an eight mile wide, twenty-three mile long ranch. Weather shifts in the mid-1870s caused another drought damaging the sheep industry, and the shift to agriculture in the region began.

Anaheim, a small German community started in 1858, began looking for a harbor from which to ship agricultural goods in 1860. They requested the US Coast Survey to examine the outlet of the Santa Ana river.

"The lagoon was found to be some five miles long and separated from the ocean by a narrow strip of sand-beach, over which the heavy southeast and northwest swells wash in every gale. The outlet or mouth is 50 yards in width, with a narrow bar outside. Over this bar there is a frightful swell, rolling and tumbling at all stages of the tide, making it dangerous to cross in boats of any kind."

Captain Greenwell, US Coast Survey, 1861

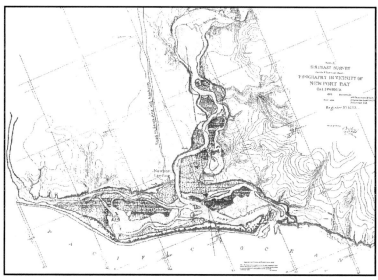

Coastal survey map of Newport Bay - 1875.
Courtesy of the Sherman Library

Although the harbor then resembled the Newport harbor that exists today, the good citizens of Anaheim bypassed the rough waters of that open bay. Instead they initiated their *Anaheim Landing* near what is now Seal Beach.

Yet in 1863, at the harbor of the Rancho San Joaquin, Captain Samuel S. Dunnels brought the *Vaquero* into the upper bay. This was a 120 foot rear-wheel steamer from San Diego, carrying lumber from up north. Captain Dunnels traded for wool, hides and grain, and with the high tide, sailed out again.

Upon a later visit, Dunnels built a short pier just north of where the Coast Highway bridge is today. He and his partner D. M. Dormann, constructed a warehouse at the pier on the west side of the upper bay.

James Irvine was in San Francisco at the time, and upon hearing of the success of the *Vaquero,* hurried back to southern California. The name Newport, according to some records, was suggested by James Irvine's personal secretary Mrs. Perkins. The *Vaquero* continued to bring lumber in from the north to the new, *Newport Landing.*

Model of The Vaquero
Courtesy of Newport Beach Nautical Museum

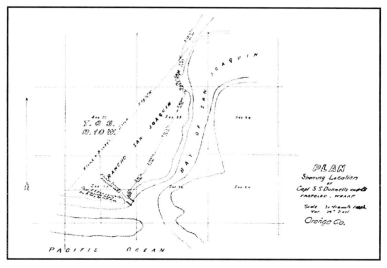

Map of Dunnels Landing.
Courtesy of the Sherman Library

Yet in 1872, the *Einora,* a sailing schooner, grounded on the bar at the mouth of the harbor, lost her anchor, and eventually was broken up by the waves. This created apprehension about using the harbor, but changes were coming with the increase in population. The end of the American Civil War brought people west to southern California, many of them Southerners.

The open range fencing law came into effect during 1873; barbed wire and fence posts were needed in great quantity to surround the vast ranch lands. James and Robert McFadden contracted with Dunnels the following year, to bring more lumber into the harbor from San Francisco. After seeing the profits from that one sale, the McFadden brothers bought the *Vaquero* and the landing.

Two years later, the McFaddens bought their own steamer, the *Newport,* and obtained the old wharf, calling it McFadden landing. They had made a deal with the Irvine Ranch, to be able to use the land for their operations, but a disagreement ensued, along with a five year lawsuit.

James Irvine died in 1886. In his will, land he had owned in San Francisco was deeded to the city for the present day civic center, along with the land for most of Golden Gate Park. Irvine left his vast ranch in southern California in the hands of trustees. They tried to sell, but James Irvine II eventually kept the ranch and incorporated it into The Irvine Company.

The McFaddens had obtained the southern part of the adjacent Rancho Santiago de Santa Ana, and in 1888, they moved their operations to the ocean side, building a wharf and later a railroad out onto a pier. A town formed, and it grew into the City of Newport Beach.

Newport Beach was quite a town by 1900. Buildings lined the pier and shore, and tall ships graced the bay and the wharf. It was becoming a city with homes and businesses, all

James Irvine II (1867-1947)
Courtesy of The Irvine Museum

generated by the shipping industry started by the McFaddens. But the McFaddens had sold out — the Southern Pacific had raised their rates, and the port of San Pedro had obtained federal recognition.

On the other side of the bay from Newport, was Rocky Point. A few ships had landed here in severe storms, so the name had meaning, but there was little else here to attract attention. Newport however, was a bustling town and incorporated only a few years later. The pier on the ocean side of the peninsula gave access to the railroad and the shipping industry. Only the bluffs that rose above the shore at Rocky Point, gave any identity to that area, and they had nothing upon them.

Weather patterns shifted in the late 1800s, rainfall previously averaging nearly 20 inches in Orange County,

McFadden Landing, under construction.
Courtesy of the Sherman Library

dropped to a mere 12 inches by 1900. The years 1897-98-99 were all especially low, with the highest equaling not quite eight inches of rain. For an agrarian business, this spelled disaster. James Irvine II sold 706 acres to a developer for $150 an acre, to generate revenue. He wrote:

"I consider it a good sale. Almost one-fourth of the area is nothing but marshlands." — James Irvine I

Rocky Point - 1900s.
Courtesy of the Sherman Library

CHAPTER 3
A Seaside Community

In July of 1904, an advertisement offering lots in Corona del Mar, published in Santa Ana's *Daily Evening Blade.* Purchasing a 706 acre tract from The Irvine Company for nearly $106,000, George E. Hart — a developer — invested in this coastal area of bluffs and marshlands. He called this *Corona del Mar,* a crown of the sea.

George Hart, born in New Hampshire in 1859, had built a lumber mill by age 18. Over a three year period, he built two more, then sold out in 1891. Moving to Washington state, he

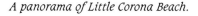

A panorama of Little Corona Beach.

CORONA DEL MAR

(FORMERLY KNOWN AS ROCKY POINT)

Santa Ana's Nearest Beach

One of the most, if not the most beautiful and attractive places-by-the-sea in Southern California. Frontage of one mile on the ocean—Two miles on the bay.

Work On Ocean Pier Commences This Week

Machinery and material for building the 600-foot ocean pier will be on the ground this week, and the work rushed to completion. Water for domestic purposes will be developed at once. Streets will be graded and oiled and an 80-foot boulevard constructed along ocean and bay front.

Maps Are Ready—Select Lots Now

Complete maps are on file with the undersigned agents. Make your selection of lots now. Prices of lots, $100 and up. Terms: One-third cash, balance easy terms to suit purchaser. Special discount to purchasers who will build.

Free Transportation

Free transportation for prospective purchasers. Purchasers of lots will be furnished with free transportation until such time as the electric road is completed to Corona Del Mar. Busses meet every train at Newport to carry passengers to Bay side where boats are ready to convey parties direct to the ground. Persons wishing to drive to Corona Del Mar can do so on Wednesdays and Saturdays, by making arrangements on the day previous with the agents.

AGENTS:

C. S. FORGY
First National Bank Building
SANTA ANA

W. B. ARTZ

TUSTIN

The first advertisement for land in Corona Del Mar, 1904.
Courtesy of the Sherman Library

entered the mill business there, and sold within five years. Moving to Oakland in northern California, Hart sold real estate for four years before moving on again. Now in Los Angeles in 1900, and after a brief shot at the oil industry in Texas, Hart established the George E. Hart & Company, a real estate firm.

Henry E. Huntington, a nephew of Collis P. Huntington (of Southern Pacific fame,) inherited some of his uncle's fortune — and then married the widow — increasing his holdings. Acquiring the Electric Railway of Los Angeles, Huntington then started the Pacific Electric Railway which reached to all corners of what was then, Los Angeles county.

Hart, in the meantime, fostered business relations with Huntington through several ventures: a Los Angeles syndicate, real estate in Long Beach, and the Newport Beach Company. Hart had obtained a one third interest in this last venture, in 1902.

The ocean side pier at Corona del Mar.
Courtesy of the Sherman Library

The Pacific Electric tracks came from Huntington Beach.
Courtesy of the Sherman Library

The Pacific Electric tracks were planned to follow the boom towns south down the coastline: Bay City (to be renamed Seal Beach,) Sunset Beach, Pacific City (renamed Huntington Beach for obvious reasons,) Newport Beach, and Balboa. All were founded between 1901 and 1906 and Hart was positioned in 1904, to benefit from the PE, when it came down the coastline.

Hart then paid a $1,000 retainer to The Irvine Company, and $9,000 ten days later. The remainder was divided into three $32,000 payments due in July of 1905, '06, & '07, at 6% interest. Effectively he had bought from what is now Jamboree to Poppy and from the East Coast Highway (& 5th) to the sea, for just $150 an acre, and $10,000 down.

The Irvine Company was very careful of their new land owner. Hart could not issue land deeds — these came directly from The Irvine Company. Also, half of the lot sales were to be credited back to the purchase, when they exceeded $5,000. Hart had to pay for half a bordering fence, and pay all taxes on the lands, beginning in July of 1905.

Of course the land would revert back to The Irvine Company if Hart failed to pay on time. As well, Hart could not mortgage the land nor allow a lien to be placed upon it, and The Irvine Company could sell adjacent lands, with only a 30 day notice to Hart. This could mean competition.

Corona del Mar then in 1904, reached from the Village to Newport Dunes, and included Irvine Terrace, Promontory Point, and Bayside. The village on the bluffs however, was the primary focus, and the land sales were only offered there.

Surveying the property into 30 foot wide lots, Hart began selling the real estate through two agents, one in Tustin and one in Santa Ana. Three on-site roads were graded: Electric Way (Bayside Drive,) Pier Avenue (Marguerite,) and Ocean Blvd. — the only street with its original name today.

Marguerite

Botanically called Chrysanthemum frutescens; frutescens means shrubby. The origin, native to the Canary Isles, they have been cultivated in England since 1699. Colour comes in white, and sometimes pink or yellow. Widely available during the summer months. Very similar to ox-eye daisies whose botanical name is Leucanthemum. These have been cultivated since 1596 and are widespread as a wild verge and hedgerow flower. Varieties are often available as small bushes or potted plants.

Per the contract and within a year, Hart had to make the following improvements at the Village:
- Plat and record the lands for sale (Village)
- Pipe in water for domestic use (from Highlands)

- Grade one mile of Ocean Blvd.
- Grade one half mile of Pier Ave. (Marguerite)
- Build two piers (at Big and Little Corona beaches)
- Oil all the roads

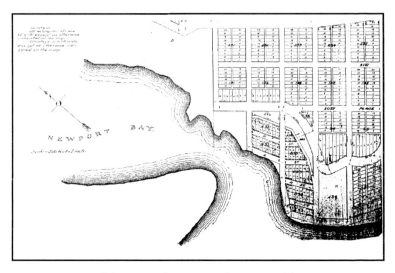

A portion of the original tract map for Corona del Mar, 1904.
Courtesy of the Sherman Library

Hart did however, gain the right to obtain water on Irvine land, first from the hills behind the community, then from the area around the San Joaquin Gun Club, the nearest establishment north of the beach area.

Lots began to sell and a 600 foot pleasure pier was started on the ocean beach. Hart began to obtain water from the hills behind Corona del Mar (per the contract with The Irvine Company,) and a launch was rented to bring people over from Balboa for free. Additionally, the Pacific Electric *(The Red Cars,)* was promised to Balboa and beyond, crossing the bay and up into the bluffs of the new community. One mile of ocean front promised an unparalleled view, and two miles of bay front offered an assurance there was a future for the new community.

The start of the 600 foot pleasure pier.
Courtesy of the Sherman Library

The bayside pier began as well. Not nearly as long as the ocean pier at 200 feet, yet necessary as transportation to the new community was presently only by boat from Balboa. Two launches were now rented for resident's use and a third was to be purchased near the end of the year. The 110 foot powered sailing yacht, the *San Diego,* was valued at some $60,000 and was to operate solely from Corona del Mar.

A tent city was platted. The lots laid out on the sand were to create a tent city, *"...equal in every way to Tent City, Coronado."* Stated George Hart. That beach today is the Corona del Mar State Beach. If there were ever any tents here in later years, they were banned by the county of Orange during the 1960s.

In this positive light, and with all that was planned, the July 13 issue of the *Daily Evening Blade* reported:

"...about thirty-five of the choicest and highest priced lots have been sold."

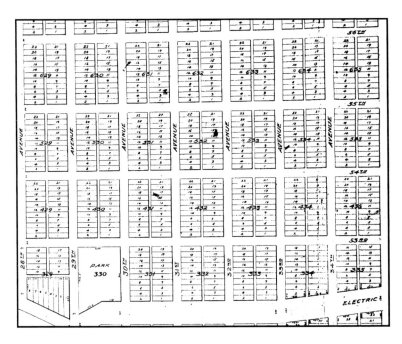

A portion of the original tract map for Corona del Mar, 1904.
Courtesy of the Sherman Library

Corona del Mar seemed an idyllic place: a romantic seaside community, with majestic bluffs, sweeping vistas, and all the benefits of city life: water, roads, and public transportation.

It was the county surveyor, Col. S.H. Finley, who had laid out the community that summer. The village was then much

Poppy

Poppies are a popular and attractive flower, common in home gardens and open fields. They come in many, many varieties, and are native to many parts of the world, including Central and Southern Europe, China, India, and other parts of Asia. Poppies are attractive and easy to grow, and come in both annual and perennial varieties. Every hue imaginable is available as well as black, and the flowers are long lasting, and Poppy seeds are used for baking. After WWII, Poppies are a symbol of both tragedy and renewal of life and gained this recognition from the many poppies in the battlefields of France. Therefore, each year Veterans sell poppies on Memorial Day, as a memorial for those who gave their lives for their country.

as it is today, only a few streets have moved, and a few more lots have been added. Finley was a civil engineer of some experience. He had laid out Pacific City (Huntington Beach,) and in Corona del Mar, created some 2,300 parcels up on the bluffs. He registered his tract map in August of that year, and had it filed the following month.

Lots were 30 feet by 118, with 18 foot wide alleyways. An 80 foot wide Ocean boulevard was promised, fronting the sea. Ocean then followed the path it does today, but Electric Way (Bayside Drive,) was wider at the time. Electric Ave. was named for the promised PE Red Car railway. It was to cross the bay and run up Pacific Gulch as Bayside does now. Pier Avenue was the primary throughway, running up from the ocean and pier. Pier ran to what was then the limit of the property, to where 5th Avenue is today.

With only three streets named, all the remainder of the streets were to be numbered, beginning with 27th (Avocado) to 43rd (Poppy.) Those parallel to the ocean were numbered as well, though beginning with 50th Place (Bayview) to 57th, which is now 5th Avenue. Street numbers were but extensions

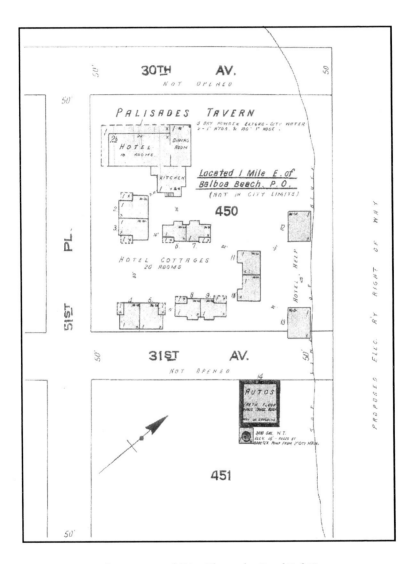

30th Avenue and 51st Place, the Hotel Del Mar.
Courtesy of the Sherman Library

of those on Balboa, and what would later become Irvine Terrace.

Water was necessary for the new community. Hart's agreement with The Irvine Company allowed him to take water in perpetuity — for domestic purposes only — from any source he could locate from up to five acres of land. Piped to the town site, water would flow at a rate of ¼ cubic foot per second.

Quoted in the August issue of the *Blade,* Hart stated:

"We've struck water at Corona del Mar. We've struck as good sweet water as you have ever tasted, and I am breathing easier."

In the canyon east of the village, 6,000 feet up Buck Gully, a crew had tapped into a good water source. Piping was being laid toward the development and water would be available soon. Several other improvements were in process besides water, such as grading and oiling the streets.

A Mission Revival bath house & pavilion was planned. Thirty dressing rooms on the first floor with a dance pavilion on the second. It was designed to rival those of other resort communities in California. This was to be a seaside resort, with beautiful vistas, boating, fishing, dancing, and swimming.

Horatio Forgy was the notary on the plat map of August 1904, obviously a relative to the sales agent in Tustin. Sales began in July — with the tract map filed in September. The real estate agents for Hart, W.B. Artz (in Tustin,) and C.S. Forgy (at Santa Ana,) began selling property: July 14, 1904, brought the first sale.

It was C.D. Ball of Santa Ana who bought just one lot. Some 60 days later he purchased three more, and E. T Ames of Los Angeles, also purchased four. Blanche E. Naylor also bought one, which brought the initial sales to nine. Blanche Naylor's lot was at Ocean and Pier.

Lots were advertised at $100, with one-third down and negotiable payments. Ball and Ames however, had bought choice properties, approaching $750 each. Their terms of sale were one-third down, one-third after a year and the remainder after two years. Other than the initial down payment however, nothing was due until two piers were up, and water was piped to the village.

The *Blade* reported that September:

"A portion of the wharf at Corona del Mar, was washed away and the remainder of it partially wrecked, the action of the breakers snapping off the piles close to the sand, as if cut with a knife."

Winter damage to the pier in 1904.
Courtesy of the Sherman Library

Rebuilding the pier began again, but another storm the following spring caused more destruction. A 600 foot pier is quite an accomplishment in 1904, without land access, and it is doubtful if this pier was ever completed.

Because of the loss of the ocean pier, the first two buyers then had cause to not make additional payments, and the eight lots were now their's. Other problems arose as the water source in Buck Gully proved to be to slight and Hart's crew was now digging for water near the San Joaquin Gun Club, north of the upper bay.

Tent City de-materialized, and existed only on a paper map. The bath house and dance pavilion never happened. The bayside pier was completed, but the ocean pier (in alignment with Pier Avenue,) continued to be pounded by the surf. Only three streets were graded, and then only onto the bluff and no further. The dream of a seaside community seemed doomed, and after only six months.

Sales only occurred that summer, and by the end of the year, no houses had been built. Hart offered up to a one-third discount on lots if a building was constructed. Still, land sales continued, if only for show. All the lots that were sold, were the nine that sold that summer; this in all of 1904.

The following year brightened a bit: 1905 began with the completion of the Balboa Pavilion and the extension of the Pacific Electric railway. This meant easy connection with the outside world; it was only an hour and a half now from Los Angeles by rail. Soon, the Red Cars were planned to reach the bluffs of Corona del Mar, and roll right up Electric Way.

The Balboa Pavilion in 1905.
Courtesy of the Sherman Library

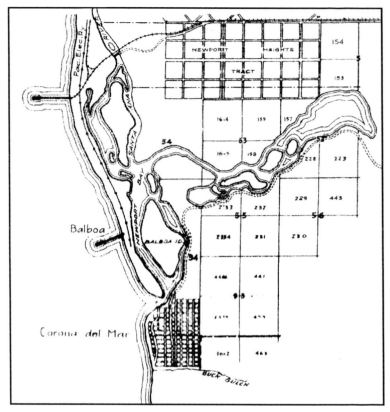

County survey map of 1912.
Courtesy of the Sherman Library

The tracks had been laid south from Huntington Beach and ran along the sand to the Pavilion, near the Balboa pier. Prospective buyers of Corona del Mar property, now could easily travel to Balboa, then hop a bus to the isthmus, where launches would — for free — take people over to the bayside pier.

This free service would continue for everyone who purchased a lot. It also applied, as per contract, to anyone purchasing a lot from the original buyers: in this case Ball and Ames. These men also specified that no one was to offer liquor for sale, in Corona del Mar. No lots were sold that year of 1905; nor in 1906. It seemed again, that the little community was due for defeat.

In that year of 1906, Hart deeded some 360 acres back to The Irvine Company for lack of payment. His village of Corona del Mar however, was saved — all 347 acres of it — little more than two sections of land.

Back Bay Drive in 1907.
Courtesy of the Sherman Library

While The Irvine Company had the right of way to build a road or run a pipeline through the property, Hart gained the right of way for:

> *"...ordinary highway purpose, reserving all rights of way thereover for railroads, street cars, telegraph and telephone lines and such like purposes..."*
> — Per the 1904 contract

Bayside Drive, as it goes up the bluffs.

Courtesy of the Sherman Library

This was from the San Joaquin Gun Club to the property, along the west line of the east bluff of the bay, 60 feet from high tide. Essentially, what is now Back Bay Drive.

In 1907 Hart built the road and a hotel. The road connected with one from Santa Ana that traveled to the San Joaquin Gun Club. This was the same area in which Hart had drilled, and found sufficient water to supply Corona del Mar for years. The article from the *Blade* then read:

"A small flow has already been found there and there is no doubt but that a sufficient quantity of excellent water will be developed for the growing needs of the coast resort."

The road then ran toward the sea and followed the upper bay. Then over to the harbor and around to the village. This road today is Back Bay Drive up until Jamboree, and then after crossing the Coast Highway, it becomes Bayside Drive. Bayside then, connected to Ocean Avenue, and went up the bluffs.

The hotel was the *Hotel Del Mar.* Three stories, 30 rooms,

The Hotel Del Mar
Courtesy of the Sherman Library

plus a dining room, kitchen, and office space. It had a large fireplace in the lobby, a ladies parlor, and was lit by gaslights. Each floor had closets, a toilet and a bathroom. That meant that each of the upper floors (of some 20 rooms,) shared the closets, toilet and bathroom. Yet, the Hotel Del Mar would provide accommodations for anyone coming to the community, and hopefully increase sales.

The hotel was located on the corner of 30th and 51st or what is now Seaview and Carnation. Bayside then went only up to Seaview as Bayside Place does today. The hotel offered majestic views of the seaside, bay, and harbor. Now with the hotel, road, pier, boats, and water, Corona del Mar could be the resort Hart wanted it to be.

Carnation

Name: Dianthus, its botanical name, means divine flower. Carnation was the flesh-pink colour Elizabethan portrait painters used as a background wash. Available in a huge range of colours
Varieties: New varieties have been bred which look like old-fashioned garden pinks, but in bright colours. They have daintier relatives, the fantastically fragrant Sweet Williams and Pinks. Folklore: Used on mothering Sunday. Language of Flowers: Red carnation for "alas for my poor heart," striped for refusal, yellow for disdain, pink for woman's love.

The hotel's builder was S.T. Hall. He was the manager for George E. Hart and Company — the same man that had built the entire Back Bay Road. Alfred Goodyear became the hotel manager when it opened of July that year. All was going well until Goodyear's sudden death by drowning a month later. This severely dampened the atmosphere in the little community.

Additional improvements came as well in 1907. A quarter

The Hotel Del Mar.
Courtesy of the Sherman Library

mile of concrete sidewalks and curbs, and another quarter mile the following year. A telephone line was brought in up to the hotel in 1908, and reached all the way to Balboa. The poles went down the bluff, and across the sand, with the wires

Telephone wires cross over the water.
Courtesy of the Sherman Library

stretching over the water. Groceries were then ordered by phone and brought over by boat. A public phone extension was available at the pier; both phones were hand-cranked. *Every modern convenience* was now available to the community.

Now Bayside Drive, the road from Back Bay to the bluffs.
Courtesy of the Sherman Library

The only store on Balboa was the *Way & Digger.* Orders by phone were carried across the bay by Captain Vallely on his launch, the *Flora.* The daily supplies were brought up the bluff by Mr. Kelly, a recluse who lived up by the water tank at Pier and 57th Ave. (Marguerite & 5th.) He eventually drowned in the bay after falling off the back of a boat — some say quite drunk.

Much of the business for the hotel came only in summer; and that mostly in meals, not room rentals. People would come out for the day, usually on weekends, but few stayed overnight. Lots still sold but few houses were built.

For the residents, transportation was limited to the long drive on the dirt road, or to cross the channel by water. Launches would tie up at the pier, waiting to take passengers across to Balboa. There, a bus would take them to the Pavilion and the P & E Railway.

The lot contracts for individuals were a bit more restricting, no building was to be used as a saloon, livery stable, or store; and no such business was to be conducted there within 30 years. Buildings were for residence use only; nor could a land owner bore or extract oil for a period up to 50 years. Houses must cost at least $2,000 to build, to be built within 15 years, and —*remembering this is 100 years ago*— not be resold to anyone of African or Mongolian descent. These were pretty hefty requirements, as any infraction or failure resulted in forfeiture of the property back to Hart.

Yet, the benefits were there. The beauty of living on the bluffs of Corona del Mar, access to the hotel, free boating to Balboa, and mail delivered and deposited at the Hotel Del Mar. Individually each lot had water piped in within 30 days at a cost of $1.25 per month and concrete curbs and sidewalks to be imminently constructed.

The Hotel Del Mar on the bluffs.
Courtesy of the Sherman Library

The year 1909 brought Mary Everett Burton to Corona del Mar. Her mother, Mary Nixon Everett and a friend, Alice Arden, had come on a pleasure visit to Newport and rented a boat for 50¢ apiece. When they saw the bluffs and the pier, they climbed up Bayside and after a day of roaming the palisades, together purchased three lots from George Hart.

Dividing the three lots in half with a stick, they now each had a 50 foot wide frontage and within the next year, built two houses. Both were board and baton construction. A board and bat house has little insulation from the weather. Boards are butted next to each other, with the narrow 'bats' covering the slits between, and shingle covering.

Mary Everett asked for a house styled after a Cape Cod design, drawn and built by a Pasadena house builder, Mr. Foss. She gave him a sketch, but he insisted upon blue prints — and a bathtub. Mary finally relented and Mr. Foss built the home in 1910, that is still there today. Mary named her summer home, *Happy House.*

Quarterdeck and Happy House in 1912.
Courtesy of the Sherman Library

Ingle Go Jang, Happy House, and Quarterdeck.
Courtesy of the Sherman Library

Alice Alden had her architect brother, Charles Arden, draw up the plans for her home next door. With the plans made, Foss ordered lumber and sent it in by rail to a siding near where Costa Mesa is today. From there, wagons brought the building materials down past the San Joaquin Gun Club, down Back Bay Drive, across Bay Front, up Bayside, to the bluffs of Corona del Mar. A crew of 22 men under Foss, built both houses within two weeks.

Furniture for the homes was purchased from Santa Ana, and had to be brought by wagons through the same path the lumber had taken. Heat was by wood and coal stoves; light came from oil lamps or candles. No gas, electricity, or roads were available, only water piped in from the tank at the top of Buck Gully.

Happy House was Mary's, the Quarterdeck was Alice's, next door. In the following year of 1911, two more houses were built to the west of Mary's and Alice's.

Mrs. Halliday and her daughter built just west of Happy House, naming their residence *Ingle Go Jang*. Dr. McLeish and his wife built west of that. Two years later, Hiram Wadsworth constructed his home east of the Quarterdeck. All were built by Foss and all of the same shingled construction, but few homes followed.

One element that brightened the decade was the film industry came to town. D. W. Griffith's earliest work on the shores of Orange County was an adaptation of a poem, *The Sands of Dee,* by Charles Kingsley back in 1912. It is the story of a Welsh girl, sent to retrieve the cattle, who disappears into the sea. Miss May Marsh was Mary, Robert Harron was Bobby, and Charles Hill Mailes starred as Mary's father.

The production company had built a house of paper-mach´, but it caught fire. One of the crew ran to the top of the bluffs to borrow a fire extinguisher, but to no avail, the paper house was destroyed. This film was a black and white silent of just 17 minutes and was filmed from Ocean Blvd. to the water.

Filming The Sands of Dee.
Courtesy of the Sherman Library

Burton house on Ocean in Corona del Mar.
Courtesy of the Sherman Library

Early summer homes in Corona del Mar.
Courtesy of the Sherman Library

Cliffs of Corona del Mar.
Courtesy of the Sherman Library

Shipping vessels had to share the harbor with pleasure boats.
Courtesy of the Sherman Library

That year, 1912, also brought aviation to Newport Harbor. The Dominguez air race in Los Angeles had fostered aviation in southern California, and Glen L. Martin had built his own aeroplane in Santa Ana. Longing to test fly it for distance, Martin succeeded in flying from the bay at Balboa to the harbor at Avalon on Santa Catalina Island. For water to water flights, it was the first, fastest, and longest. When he came back to Balboa the same day, he brought the return mail. A historical plaque is located at the land end of the Balboa pier, marking this historical achievement.

The first water to water flight, 1912.
Courtesy of the Sherman Library

Essentially, The Irvine Ranch surrounded the village of Corona del Mar, giving it the feel of the old Rancho days. Cattle roamed on the hillsides, behind and south of the bluffs, and occasionally, someone would ride by on horseback. Adults now remember collecting mushrooms as children off the bluffs on ranch land, sparking stories of wild bulls chasing them back to the safety of the barbed wire. By 1914, Corona del Mar had barely a dozen homes, after a whole decade.

A great storm hit that year and the old pier of Pier Ave. fell to the waves. It had shortened itself to less than half of its original

The trail to Rocky Point.

Courtesy of the Sherman Library

Early postcard of Rocky Point
Courtesy of the Sherman Library

600 feet and the planking was long gone. While there was no rain, the waves came right up to the bluffs, breaking the pilings as they rolled ashore. The great pier was gone, by that afternoon.

Finally by 1915, George E. Hart admitted defeat, and sold his beloved Corona del Mar. He traded it actually, for 5,000 acres in Riverside to the F.D. Cornell Company. While the isolation of the bluff top community was part of its draw, it was also its drawback. Without the Pacific Electric Railway and with limited road access, the village had grown only to 15 homes and a scattering of a few hundred lots.

George F. Hart
Courtesy of the Sherman Library

Rocky Point, Corona del Mar
Courtesy of the Sherman Library

CHAPTER 4
On Corona del Mar

The F. D. Cornell Company took over operations at Corona del Mar in 1916, but sales continued to lag. Cornell himself took it upon himself to change the name of Corona del Mar to *Balboa Palisades* and to increase advertising. Balboa had been platted in 1905, (the year after Corona del Mar), and was widely known by this time, primarily due to access by the Pacific Electric Railway. Cornell wanted to rely upon the popularity of the beach resort, to promote his town on the bluffs.

The deal that had transpired was the rescinding of the

A panorama of the Hotel Del Mar.

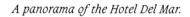

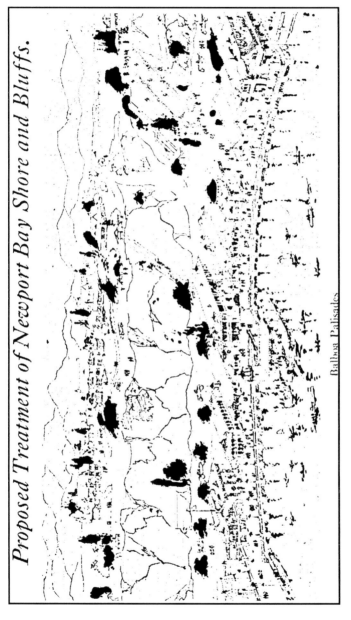

Proposed Treatment of Newport Bay Shore and Bluffs.

Balboa Palisades

Plans for Balboa Palisades

Courtesy of the Sherman Library

A staged photo, used for promotion.
Courtesy of the Sherman Library

original contract with The Irvine Company and George Hart; then a new contract awarding Hart 347 acres of the present village of Corona del Mar. This was mortgaged to a holding company and then sold to F. D. Cornell. Hart then received the lands in Riverside as compensation. All this transpired between 1915 and 1916.

Cornell tried promotion of the little town, with advertisements in newspapers, promotional postcards, anything that would garner more lot sales. The Del Mar Hotel was renamed the Palisades Tavern, to coincide

F. D. Cornell
Courtesy of the Sherman Library

with the new name of the community and Cornell built a landing to receive prospective clients at the bay side pier. Still without better access, the bluff top community grew slowly.

In addition, Cornell changed the street names. Ocean Blvd. remained, but all the other street names changed. What was the road leading from Back Bay, became Palisades Road, for the new name of the Village. Electric Way was changed to Pacific Drv., as the Red Cars were never coming. 50th became Bayview Drv., and 51st became Seaview Ave. 53rd to 57th became 1st Ave. through 5th Ave., as it is today. Pacific Drive is remembered today between Avocado and Begonia, where the remainder up Pacific Gulch, was eventually renamed Bayside Drv. which connected with Bayside on the bay.

Begonia
One of America's favorite flowers, with lots of variety. Begonias are popular in flowerbeds, for hanging baskets, as container plants, and for indoor houseplants. They are prized equally for their flower as well as their showy leaves. They make a good indoor houseplants as they tolerate shade well.
Types: There are three types of Begonias: Tuberous, Semperflorens, and the uncommon Perennials. The Semperflorens are by far the most common. They include Fibrous Begonias, Wax Begonias and Everblooming Begonias. Depending upon type, you can find red, white, pink, or yellow varieties. All flowers have a bright yellow eye(center).

All the other street names were changed to flowers: From Acacia, to Poppy, in alphabetical order. Avocado didn't exist yet and neither did Hazel. Pansy was an afterthought, as there already was a "P" street and Pansy later was changed to Poinsettia, and there were never any 'E' or 'K' streets. Then Pier Ave. was changed to Marguerite, making two 'M' streets

The pier finally fell in 1914.
Courtesy of the Sherman Library

as well. The Coast Highway wasn't thought of yet, but was later planned to go through 5th Ave.

All of this effort was for not, as the number of homes even by the 1920s was never above 50. Cornell, to say the least was persistent, and his marketing tactics went as far as a general plan for the seaside community — including a bath house — and a new pier and landing, which was built in 1917.

A jetty was started in back in 1917, on the western side of the channel. The first rock, thrown into the water was celebrated on September 10th, with a full band.

The jetty was constructed though an open frame pier, first built out into the open water. The Pacific Electric line was extended out onto the pier, to bring out the rock. The rail line and pier were later removed.

The jetty somewhat protected the harbor, but started the decline of large waves at Big Corona beach. The waves now had a smooth rolling effect, which irritated the surfers. The jetty was continually damaged due to storms, which allowed the continued surfing at Big Corona.

During the teens and twenties, Corona del Mar became a draw, not for residents, but for the movie industry. As early as 1912, directors and producers began using the dramatic seaside as backdrops for their films.

Building the pier, to build the jetty- 1927.
Courtesy of the Newport Harbor Nautical Museum

Throwing the first rock - 1927.
Courtesy of the Newport Harbor Nautical Museum

Building the jetty while the band played on. - 1927.
Courtesy of the Newport Harbor Nautical Museum

Building the jetty - 1927.
Courtesy of the Newport Harbor Nautical Museum

David Wark Griffith (D.W.), was the most prolific film director of all time. He directed over 500 films, writing over 200 of those, as well as produced, acted and was otherwise involved in an additional 50 movies. He directed films in San Juan Capistrano as early as 1910, and was attracted to the rugged coastline of Orange County. Griffith was soon filming regularly on Corona del Mar.

Many of these were film shorts, one reelers up to 20 minutes long, and could be produced and released in as little as 30 days. Many were made back-to-back, and 1916 was a banner year. Films were all black and white silents, up until the first 1927 talkies — color came only a dozen years later.

The Lash, a father and son power-play drama of 1916, starred Marie Doro, Elliott Dexter and James Neill; was filmed down by Cameo Shores. Directed by James Young, this black

The witches cauldron at Pirates Cove.
Courtesy of the Sherman Library

and white silent was exceedingly long: 4½ reels or 90 minutes.

In this story, a father is proud of being a self-made man while his son is a lazy playboy, of which the father is far from happy. He's worked hard to earn his money and his power, and doesn't want his son to squander it away. Henry Starck, a local fisherman, was paid $100 to capsize a dory boat through Arch Rock.

This was followed by *Macbeth* in the same year. Shakespeare's tragedy of a Scottish nobleman, starred Sir Herbert Beerbohm Tree, Constance Collier, and Wilfred Lucas. It was directed by John Emerson, but produced again by D. W. Griffith through Triangle-Fine Arts. The most notable element of this film is that the witches were played by men in drag: L. Tylden, Scott McKee, and Jack Leonard. Pirate's cove was used as the witches hideout.

Production scaffolding for the movie Treasure Island.
Courtesy of the Sherman Library

Cleopatra barge sailing up the Nile.

Courtesy of the Sherman Library

Sir Herbert Beerbohm Tree was well known for his portrayal of Macbeth on stage, so was brought into the film to record his performance. Stuffy and overbearing, Tree had to have everything his way. When filming, he felt the camera was in the way of his performance and also spoke all of the dialogue. The director would then shoot just what he needed and then remove the film from the camera — ordering the cameraman to keep cranking until Tree was through. Unfortunately, this film of Macbeth is now lost.

Cleopatra was also filmed in 1916 (but released the following year,) as the story of the Queen of Egypt and her epic romance with Julius Caesar and Antony. J. Gordon Edwards directed famed actress Theda Bara, along with Frits Leiber and Thurston Hall as the Caesars. Cleopatra's galley could be seen floating up the harbor.

The famed Battle of Actium was held in the upper bay, with the fight ensuing to the point that the sailors had to jump ship. The extras who were hired to do the job however, wouldn't jump. Apparently one who had, stepped on a ray and was stung.

The storm tossed sea, for the Sea Wolf.
Courtesy of the Sherman Library

The stage is set for Treasure Island.

Courtesy of the Sherman Library

That stopped the production, until Edwards offered more money for each man, then the show was on and the battle continued.

Julius Caesar (Frits Leiber) had a scene with his chariot but the horses bolted and ran up the bluff. When finally stopped, Frits was crying and emotionally unnerved. This was one of the longest films of its time: over two hours.

In November of 1919, *The Sea Wolf,* was produced by Famous Players and starred Noah Beery, Raymond Hatton and Mabel Julienne Scott. A Jack London sea-soaker, this was a tragic story that required special shooting requirements for the storm scenes. A water camera rig was set up to shoot the ship, rolling into the harbor.

> *"The Village was erected at Crystal Cove, and the storm staged on Newport Harbor."*
>
> Jim Sleeper's *Shot in Orange County*

Producers took advantage of the storms along the coast, by shooting in the winter time and rather short: one to two months at the most. Most crews stayed at the Palisades Tavern.

Hobart Bosworth did the remake of *The Sea Wolf*, and had the movie rights to all of Jack London's books. Bosworth had starred in his own 1913 version of this film and now staged this production at Corona Del Mar and had the crew staying, and drinking, at the Palisades Tavern. The production ran into 1920; pro-

Film poster of Tarzan

hibition had begun that January.

Charles Clarke, pioneer cameraman for the National Film Corporation in the 1920s, shot the 15 part serial *The Son of Tarzan* (1920) at Corona del Mar. He later wrote:

> *"We were filming an episode of 'The Son of Tarzan,' and needed a primitive shoreline-palisades area where Tarzan could come ashore. There was no Coast Highway then, so after a long drive around the head of the bay, we finally arrived at Corona del Mar. As I remember, there was only one frame building on the headland overlooking the harbor entrance — a sort of tavern, where our little crew put up."*

First release of Chapter One was in December of 1920 and *The Son of Tarzan* was largely shot in Corona del Mar. Kamuela C. Searle (Boy) died filming chapter 15 when an elephant stepped on him.

Other films of note were produced here, *The Count of Monte Cristo* in 1922 and no less than three versions of Robert Louis

Bootleggers brought liquor up the bluffs during the 1930s.
Courtesy of the Sherman Library

Bayside Drive as it turns into Electric Way.
Courtesy of the Sherman Library

Stevenson's classic tale, *Treasure Island*. This was filmed down the coast at Crystal Cove, but the crews stayed in Corona del Mar. Possibly in 1912 and for sure in 1917, the last version filmed here was in 1937, starring Wallace Beery, a young Jackie Cooper and Lionel Barrymore.

Prohibition started on the 29th of January 1920, and lasted to the end of 1933 — some 13 years. Preventing liquor from being manufactured or sold in the US, this time period gave rise to black market alcohol. As liquor became scarce in the southland, covert operations brought many rumrunners to the area. Before 1916, a dirt road had been completed from Corona del Mar to Laguna. Crystal Cove, only a scant mile away, supplied a place well hidden from outsiders for bootleggers.

Liquor boats were painted black and would moor off the shore, where cars along the bluffs would signal, by flashing their lights. The rumrunners would then smuggle in their cargo. Years later people walking the same beach would discover old liquor bottles poking out of the sand.

F. D. Cornell gave up quicker that George Hart had. Cornell sold the remaining lots and hotel to W. S. Sparr in 1922, a Los

Sparr's Bath House, China House, Kerchkhoff Marine Lab, and the weather station on the bluff.
Courtesy of American First Title Insurance

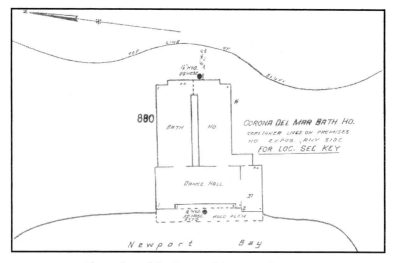

Floor plan of the Corona del Mar Bath House.
Courtesy of the County Archives

Angeles fruit packer. Sparr was another land speculator, but
then most of the people who bought lots were land speculators.
They bought the land, just to see if the value would go up. Few
came to live here and most of those were here only for summer.

The Corona del Mar Bath House was built in the early 1920s
by Sparr, as a part of the hotel. It was located below the hotel,
that had been constructed years before. The Bath House came
with a changing area, a dance hall, offices, and a large wooden
porch. Later it was known as Sparr's Bath House. It had been
built high off the water on pilings, and gave pleasure to people
for many years, until it burned in the early 1930s.

Quietly, in the winter of 1923, a vote was held to decide to
incorporate Corona del Mar into the City of Newport Beach.
Those living in Newport Beach were for it with a vote of 181
to 37. Voting in winter meant that there were only seven winter
residents of Corona del Mar available, which were for the vote
as well. Cityhood for the village, meant services to the
community and a big bonus: good water. This took effect in

Aerial view of the few buildings on the bluff.
Courtesy of the Sherman Library

1924, 20 years after the original founding of the Village. Not much changed, except for the addition of two streets: Avocado and Hazel — at the opposite ends of the Village.

Lots were then assessed the following year, at $100 each for the most part. In total all the structures were valued at $5,700. Still, there weren't many homes, and no businesses on the bluff. The City Council of Newport Beach, always referred to the Village, as "On Corona del Mar."

The boom that finally came to Corona del Mar, was not from promotion, nor cityhood, nor good water, but transportation. The Coast Highway had long been planned to

---

Fernleaf Goldthread
Fernleaf and fernleaf yarrow are from the genus Achillea filipendulina. Their perennial life span is three to ten years and their overall height is from three to four feet.

Heliotrope
Heliotrope is one of the most ancient of flowers. In modern aesthetics it stands for art and good taste. It is thought to be the flower to which Clytie was changed when she died of love for glorious Apollo.

run from Long Beach to the paved roadway below San Juan Capistrano, connecting all the beach cities. Forty feet wide and six to seven inches thick, the concrete for the highway was poured in segments that took 28 days each just to cure. The cost to build the highway was $9,500 a mile.

In Corona del Mar, the street easement was 80 feet, which allowed for expansion in the future. The Coast Highway, was slated to follow 5th Ave. to Poppy, but was rerouted to it's present diagonal at the request of the City,

Curbs were poured, but not yet the street for Coast Highway.
Courtesy of the Sherman Library

to encourage lot sales.

On October 9th in Laguna Beach, a chain of flowers was carried by a representative bathing beauty from each coastal city: Laguna Beach, Newport Beach, Huntington Beach, Sunset Beach, Seal Beach, and Long Beach. Commonly called Pacific Coast Highway, the road opened with Mary Pickford & Douglas Fairbanks officiating.

The famous couple 'tied the knot,' rather than 'cut the ribbon.' This symbolized the joining of the beach communities, along the southern California shoreline. They had married inside the old Mission at San Juan Capistrano a few years before, having made several movies at the now famous Mission. One of Fairbanks features shot there, was the first of the Zorro films.

Mary Pickford & Douglas Fairbanks tied the knot.
Courtesy of the First American Title Insurance

The new highway brought people in droves. Affectionately called *'Coast Highway'* in Corona del Mar, it is titled West and East Coast Highway, separating at the bridge in Newport Beach.

Duke Kahanamoku.
Courtesy of Viola - Aquatic Champion

More cars with visitors stopped at Corona del Mar and invaded the beaches. The two beaches, to be called Big Corona and Little Corona, became popular to beach goers and the surfing crowd. Surfing was new to California.

Duke Kahanamoku was Hawaiian: the last of his royal line. He had made his mark in the 1912 Olympics, winning the 50 yard freestyle in 25-4.5. He was by far, the fastest man in the water. The Duke came to California and was coached by Fred Cady at the Los Angeles Athletic Club.

He introduced two remarkable things to the mainland. He brought his long and powerful swimming stroke referred to as *The Australian Crawl* and he introduced the long wooden

Duke Kahanamoku with Viola Hartmann on the shores of Orange County.
Courtesy of Viola - Aquatic Champion

surfboard. Both made him famous.

By 1925 however, the Palisades Tavern had been sold, and became the Balboa Palisades Beach Club. Big Corona was considered one of the best surfing spots in California. It drew the best surfers and large crowds, and the mainland's first surfing association was the Corona del Mar Surfboard Club. Contests were held and the Pacific Coast Surf Riding Championships were formed in 1928 by Tom Blake. He

National Champion Surfing Contest 1928.
Courtesy of the Sherman Library

established the championships through the Surfboard Club.

Although the Duke was invited, for some reason he did not participate. This left Tom to be the favored competitor and gave him a chance to prove his ability. The course was to a buoy, 500 yards off shore. Everyone paddled out and rode the waves back. With only 15 entries, people on the shore could follow their surf rider.

Tom won, but only with a unique method. He took out two boards. The bottom one was a standard heavy paddleboard, but the top one was a lighter surfboard. At the turn of the buoy, Tom dropped the heavier board, and rode in on the lighter one, easily winning the race.

Another National Surfing Champion came from Orange County: Keller Watson Jr. He held the title in the 1930s, until he took over his fathers' store up in Orange. Watson's Drug

1928 Surfing Competition at Corona del Mar.
Courtesy of the Sherman Library

Surfing increased because of the west jetty.
Courtesy of the Sherman Library

Store today, is still going after a century of operation. The surfing competitions continued on until they were stopped by WWII.

Surfing increased in popularity throughout the United States coastal areas, but only with the early efforts of the Surfboard Club at Corona del Mar.

The east jetty may have slowed the wave action, but the east Jetty created the Wedge, a surfing haven (or nightmare.) the Wedge to this day, is know for it's brutal waves.

During the 1920s and '30s, storms (and the west jetty,) caused a number of ships to wreck on or near the harbor entrance. Actually, offshore of Orange County, some three dozen ships met their doom.

The *Muriel,* came to life in 1895 up in San Francisco bay as a four masted schooner, and plied the pacific as a lumber trader to southern California. Breifly used in the motion picture industry, it now had a lowly life as a fishing barge.

The Muriel grounded between the jetties in 1928. Courtesy of the Sherman Library

A 537 tonne vessel, the *Muriel* had been converted into a barge by cutting off the masts at the deck. This was common at the time, for the old sailing vessels had become obsolete. One mast is still in the harbor, as a pier off Balboa Island.

As the ship was being towed out of the harbor in July of 1926, the lines broke and the old ship became stranded on a sandbar. Considered a navigation hazard, the Federal government hired Captain Eliason to remove the remains.

Eliason moved the ship to the sandbar adjacent to the west jetty early the next year. (He also brought out an 18 foot octopus from the hold.) Now clear of the main channel, the ship remained there for three years.

A family exploring the grounded Muriel.
Courtesy of the Sherman Library

The construction of the Goldenrod Footbridge - 1928.
Courtesy of the Sherman Library

Workman on the Goldenrod Footbridge - 1928.
Courtesy of the Sherman Library

Goldenrod

Goldenrod is classified in the sunflower family as Solidago, Compositae. Of about 130 species in North America, the perennial herbs bloom in late summer or early autumn. Related to the aster, it typically has a slender, unbranched stem, with short-stalked or even stalkless leaves. Small, yellow flower heads in clusters give it the name. Widespread throughout the United States, goldenrod has been erroneously blamed for the hayfever caused by ragweed (Ambrosia).

A new contract to remove the *Muriel* was given to two other men, who burned the hull to the water line, dynamited the remains, and pulled the debris ashore. A truck was then hired to haul the remains away, and in 1930, a dredge removed the sand bar, clearing the channel.

The *Esther Buhne,* an 1887 schooner barge, stranded at the end of Balboa peninsula during a storm. After it broke up, all the timber drifted south to Crystal Cove, where the enterprising residents utilized the find in making cottages. Most of Cabin #9, was made from that ship. The *Yours Truly,* a gas yawl of 1930, burned to the water line near Corona del Mar in 1934. Five years later, the *Paragon,* an oil yawl, stranded itself on the Balboa peninsula.

Up on the bluff however, house lots were slow to sell even in the 1920s (and especially in the 1930s.) The City of Newport Beach then built a footbridge across Pacific Gulch at Goldenrod to help sales. It was designed to make lots on the inland side of Bayside Drive, 'beach lots,' but sales slowly improved.

In August of 1928, the Goldenrod Footbridge was completed. The 240 foot long concrete bridge, cost almost $11,000, and had three support pylons each 30 feet tall. At six feet wide, the bridge was built over the course of four months.

Office of realtor, Kenneth I. Fulton.
Courtesy of the Sherman Library

Corona del Mar in the 1930s on Coast Highway.
Courtesy of the Sherman Library

On Corona del Mar

The west jetty, built in 1917 and continually reinforced over the years.
Courtesy of the Sherman Library

The Newport News reported:

> *"The two sections on either side of Pacific Canyon are accessible at last. It gives dwellers on the North and East side, a walk of less than 10 minutes to the beach. No more terrible down the stony and gravel trail of the gulch. We are all pleased indeed."*

Noting the isolated use of the term Pacific Canyon, instead of gulch, the not so famous Buck Gully was once unofficially renamed *Ca ˜yon del Buca,* by Kenneth I. Fulton. He was a local realtor, who printed a sales map in the 1920s, showing the name of Buck Gully in Spanish.

A shorter version of its cousin, the east jetty began construction in 1928. It protected the harbor too, and was planned to stretch out as far as the west jetty, but was not completed until 1936.

The two jettys of Newport Harbor

Courtesy of the Sherman Library

Ladies enjoy the seashore at Corona del Mar.
    Courtesy of the Sherman Library

The Palisades Club.

Courtesy of the Sherman Library

CHAPTER 5
Depression and the War Years

Pleasure boating grew in popularity. With the Newport marina building up, more weekend boaters took to the sea. Shipping was still in process at the harbor, so boaters had to share the waterway.

Mail had always been delivered to the Hotel Del Mar, now the Palisades Club. In 1926, a post office was started up, in a local store on Coast Highway and Marigold. Chris and Edna Stukey ran the shop, Edna was Postmistress. The store changed hands (and postmasters,) into the 1930s.

A panorama of China Cove.

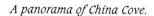

In 1929, an unusual house was constructed over what became known as *'China Cove,'* called by all as the *'China House,'* because of it's styling. Built by department store tycoon, William Lindsay. A grand feature for many years, the China House sported a tiled, oriental roofline, ornate interior fixtures and a carved dragon, to greet visitors. The China House remained until 1987.

The Balboa Palisades Club was started in 1926 by a group of some 100 individuals from Pasadena. They invisioned a prestigious bath house, surrounded by private cottages. The corner stone was set in October of 1925 with a host of celebrities including Duke Kahanamoku and Dorothy Mackaill, a film star of First National Pictures. Although Dorothy's career spanned only 17 years, she had made 65 films when she retired at the age of 34.

The Great Depression came at the end of 1929. Lot sales plummeted and many land owners just gave up their lots to the City of Newport Beach, for a mere $75 in back taxes. The City then offered lots at bargain basement prices; still, few were

China House built in 1929.
Courtesy of the Sherman Library

Coastline view of the China House.
Courtesy of the First American Title Insurance

Pleasure boating in front of the China House.
Courtesy of the Newport Harbor Nautical Museum

sold, even into the 1940s.

The California Institute of Technology (Caltech,) started its division of Biology in 1928. At the beginning of the Great Depression, William G Kerckhoff funded the purchase (at $50,000) and renovation of the Balboa Palisades Club. Creating the Kerckhoff Marine Lab in 1929, a second wing was added in 1938. The Lab studies the behavior of marine life.

An underwater tunnel was actually started in 1931, below the harbor channel. The eventual failure and collapse of the venture was due in part, to the 1933 Long Beach earthquake.

In the late afternoon of March 10th, 1933, the infamous Long Beach earthquake hit with a disastrous effect — in Long Beach. The epicenter however, was but five miles north of Corona del Mar, and a mile out at sea, the greatest damage reported was of course, up in Long Beach.

The Inglewood faultline runs from about a mile out in the oceans, from the mouth of the Santa Ana river, up through

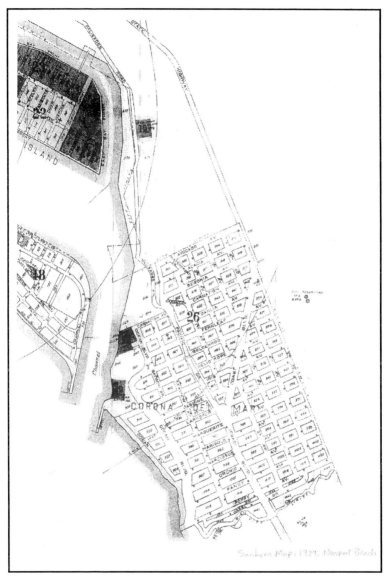

Map showing the Village and the location of the Palisades Club.
Courtesy of the Sherman Library

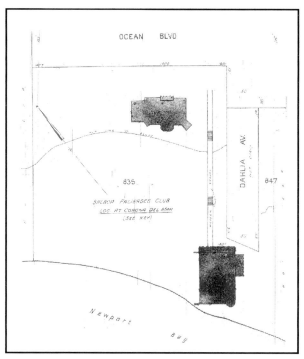

Map of Palisades Club House.
Courtesy of the Sherman Library

Palisades Club House and pier.
Courtesy of the Sherman Library

Balboa Palisades Club being built in the background - 1926.
Courtesy of the Sherman Library

Tail O' the Cock now Five Crowns Restaurant.
Courtesy ofthe Sherman Library

Pleasure boat crosses in front of the Bath House.
Courtesy of the Newport Harbor Nauticle Museum

Silouette of the China House.
Courtesy ofHoward Folsom

Long Beach and turns north through Inglewood. Little damage if any was reported in the Village, mostly because so few buildings were actually there.

A year later in 1934, the city dredged the harbor to a depth

Marine Lab is shown at the right of picture.
Courtesy of the Sherman Library

All Quiet on the Western Front, at Corona del Mar.
Courtesy of the Sherman Library

of 25 feet. Both jetties were reinforced with 200,000 tons of rock, and the east jetty was extended to 1,700 feet. Completed in 1936, this and the eventual removal of the sandbar at the entrance to the harbor, ended the waves at the beaches.

Films continued to be produced at Corona del Mar, even during the great depression. A famous film made in Corona del Mar in 1929 was *All Quiet on the Western Front.* Directed by Lewis Milestone, it is a WWI story of German schoolboys who enlist at the start of the war. Told through their eyes, the story shows all the horror and death of war. Starring Louis Wolheim, Lew Ayres, John Wray, and Arnold Lucy, this Oscar winning film was adapted from a German Novel. A black and white, mono sound picture, the film ran 131 minutes and was banned in Germany from it's inception through 1945. It was largely shot where Harbor View is today.

In 1934, Wanda Nimmo bought the grocery store that then held the Post Office and called it Wanda's. She too held the Postmistress title and started a lending library as well. Three years later, Wanda got married and left the job to Mrs. Anderson, and the office then moved in 1940. Here it stayed until the 1950s.

Matilda Lemon MacCulloch bought property in Corona del Mar in the 1930s. She had been to Santa Monica years before and adored the coastline. In her travels to England, she discovered a tavern, *'Ye Old Bell,'* at Hurley on the Thames, west of London. Taken by it's architecture, (and the claim of the year of

Aerial view of the harbor prior to dredging.
Courtesy of the Sherman Library

1135,) upon return to southern California, she hired an architect. Her desire was to duplicate the old inn as a house, and she called it the Hurley Bell, in honor of it's English origin. The home was completed in 1936 on Coast Highway at Poppy, at a cost of $10,000.

U.S. Post Office - 1940.
Courtesy of the Sherman Library

Tillie (Matilda) moved in with her daughter Marguerite and lived there four years. In 1940, she was approached by two men to open a restaurant. Leasing the building, Shelton McHenry and Bruce Warren opened the Tail O' The Cock. Gambling ensued at the restaurant, and the partners broke up within three years.

Tillie and Marguerite moved back to the area and reopened the

Matilda Lemon MacCulloch.
Courtesy of the Sherman Library

Ye Olde Bell at Hurley on the Thames, in England.
Courtesy of the Sherman Library

The Hurley Bell, on Corona del Mar.
Courtesy of the Sherman Library

Hurley Bell as an inn — sort of a bed-and-breakfast of the times. The little inn became a hideaway for Hollywood celebrities. Howard Hughes, Rita Hayworth, Peter Lorree, Lana Turner, Bette Davis, Ava Gardner, Humphery Bogart, and Lauren Bacall, were just some of the socialites. Tillie died in 1948 and Marguerite married soon after. The Hurley Bell was leased out to several restaurants over the years.

During the depression, sales of Corona del Mar lots and homes continued, although slowly. Realtor John Sherrod Harris in 1937, produced a large, multi-page brochure, which represented Corona del Mar well — a 100 foot water front property was offered at $11,500 — quite a price for the 1930s.

Different 'Units' were offered for sale: units one & two were sand and bluff lots facing the bay; unit three had sand and bluff lots facing the ocean; unit four was above Ocean Blvd with lots and new houses. Sand lots went for a mere $850; the office was located on Larkspur where S. W. Whitcher, the sales agent could be found.

Quarterdeck, one of the first houses on Corona del Mar.

Presently, on the coastal lands of the Irvine Ranch, Japanese farmers worked the land. A dozen or more families leased from The

UNIT TWO

OUR
TRACT
SALESMAN

At His Station
"Ask Him"

THIS STATION
Is at Foot of
Ramp as Shown
in Unit Two
"Ask Him"

A View of a Portion of Unit Two

WE SAY—IF YOU ARE GOING TO BUY A BEACH SITE
"BUY SOMEWHERE IN NEWPORT BEACH"

NATURALLY, WE HOPE YOU WILL LOOK OVER OUR PROPERTIES IN
C O R O N A   D E L   M A R

BEFORE MAKING YOUR DEFINITE DECISION AS TO WHAT AND WHERE YOU WILL BUY.
WE RECOMMEND THAT YOU CONSIDER CAREFULLY ALL THE ADVANTAGES AND DIS-
ADVANTAGES OF EACH LOCATION—THEN BUY THAT WHICH SUITS YOU BEST.

View of Another Portion of Unit Two

Advertisement of the 'Units' for sale on Corona del Mar - John Harris.
Courtesy of the Sherman Library

Houses during the depression on Corona del Mar.
Courtesy of the Sherman Library

Irvine Company, and dry farmed, relying on infrequent rainfall and the moisture from the sea to grow their crops. They used trucks to plow the land, which created the term 'truck farming.' Bush-beans, peas, and Kentucky wonder beans could be seen for sale along the roadside stands on the Coast Highway.

President Franklin D. Roosevelt's motorcade in 1938.
Courtesy of the Sherman Library

The bluffs of Corona del Mar.
Courtesy of the Sherman Library

Motorists after 1926, traveling the highway, bought bags of vegetables, up to the 1940s. During harvest time, the farmers took three truckloads a day, to the LA markets. Only some of the farmers did well. Dry farming is a risky business and they used no fertilizers or pesticides. After the harvest, the vines would be plowed back into the ground, to replenish the nitrogen in the soil.

A schoolhouse for regular school, was on the inland side of Coast Highway, about a mile south of Corona del Mar. The school, known as *San Joaquin #2,* was for both Japanese and caucasian children. After the eighth grade however, all the students were bussed first to Corona del Mar, and then over the Newport Bay bridge to Newport Harbor High School.

Homes and barns were built to accommodate the families and their farming needs. The farm lands were leased from The Irvine Company, and the barns and houses eventually became part of the ranch operation. Only one structure exists today.

A Japanese schoolhouse, for Saturday Japanese studies, was located on the coast side of the highway, south of Corona del Mar. There, they were taught Japanese customs, religion and language.

Japanese farmers on Irvine land during the 30s.
Courtesy of the Sherman Library

After the bombing of Pearl Harbor, in December of 1941, Japanese citizens residing in the United States, and American citizens of Japanese descent were relocated to one of ten internment camps. The farmers of the Irvine coast, lost their homes and all of their belongings. The Japanese school is now Cabin #45 at Crystal Cove.

A state wide blackout occurred after the bombing of Pearl Harbor. Only one other major incident occurred throughout the war, in southern California. The greatest fear was of the possibility the Japanese would bomb the coastline, including the peninsula. Air raid wardens were selected and the region was divided up with each warden responsible for a given area. Blackouts were mandatory at night and headlights on cars were painted blue, or had masks placed over the lens, with thin slits to emit light.

In early 1942, anti-aircraft guns blazed into the night over Santa Monica bay during an air raid. Searchlights criss-crossed in the sky looking for enemy aircraft, but none could be found. The next day showed the only successful 'hits' by Americans were the bombing of a fishing barge and the torpedoing of a lumber freighter off Point Vicente. Known as the 'Battle of Santa Monica', the newspapers had a field day with this story.

In the quiet village of Corona del Mar however, the few homes were protected by the artillery guns that were stationed at Long Point on Palos Verdes. Little affected the Village, other than war rationing and the other inconveniences of the times.

When the war ended, all was quite on the bluffs. Soon, that was about to change.

Aerial view during the depression.
Courtesy of the Sherman Library

View of the jetties after the war.

Courtesy of the Sherman Library

CHAPTER 6
The Village Grows

After the war ended, the service men and women came back; 16 million of them. Their return, (many to the Los Angeles area,) created the greatest housing boom in the history of America. Starting in 1946, more than 10,000 babies were born in the U.S., each and every day — for over two decades.

Still, conditions were considerably primitive: busses ran only twice a day, telephones were 8-party lines, and a good steak was $2.00. Of course that included soup, salad, dessert and coffee.

A panorama of the bluffs, from above the reservoir

The 1950s entrance to Corona del Mar
Courtesy of Howard Folsom

Harbor Photo Lab in 1946.
Courtesy of Howard Folsom

The year 1946 found Glen Couch opening his photography shop on the Coast Highway. He was joined the next year by Howard Folsom, who lived in the Village. Glen left a year later, and Howard took over the store. Harbor Photo Lab is the oldest business in Corona del Mar — and with just one owner.

The Irvine Company sought to develop Big Corona beach, but through the tireless efforts of Mary Burton, the land was acquired by the State of California, and became Corona del Mar State Beach in 1947. Two years later, the California State Park Commission revised the shoreline, making the State beach such as it is today.

The first school opened in 1948: the Corona del Mar Elementary School, taking up the two block area from 2nd to 4th, and Carnation to Dahlia. The janitor lived across

Advertising for the city of Corona del Mar.
Courtesy of Howard Folsom

Harbor Photo Lab in 1965.
Courtesy of Howard Folsom

the street from the school.

That year, the first bank in Corona del Mar opened through a permit from the California State Banking Committee. This provided the financial support necessary to grow the business district along Coast Highway. The Silhouette Shop opened, offering ladies lingerie and in 1949, the Corona del Mar Improvement Association was established.

The Shell Oil company began oil drilling on the highlands above the Village. Located outside the original 700 acres of George Hart, it would have invalidated the contractual agreement which stipulated no oil drilling would be allowed for 50 years — and just four years shy.

Snow fell for the only time in the recorded history of Corona del Mar in 1949. School was out, roads were closed, and Orange County was blanketed with white for just a day.

Snow on Corona del Mar - 1949!

Photos courtesy of Howard Folsom

Back Bay in snow, San Joaquin Hill in the distance.

Courtesy of Howard Folsom

Dahlia

Dahlias are native to Mexico and South America, and have the vibrant intense colors associated with that part of the world. The native forms are simple and daisy-like, but breeding has resulted in wonderful flower forms, including globes full of petals (pompoms), spiky and spidery forms (cactuses), and curled tubes of petals like sea anemones. Dahlias were first discovered in 1615, and were called by the, acoctli. Rediscovered in 1787 by a botanical expedition who sent seeds back to Europe. Their existence was kept secret for over ten years.

The Post Office up until this time, had been a pick up only facility. It was proudly announced that with $40,000 in receipts in 1949, regular mail delivery would begin in Corona del Mar. Throughout the United States in 1950, the U.S. Post Office began 'corrections' of Post Office names and closed the *Corona Del Mar* office, reopening it as the

Opening day of the Corona del Mar Post Office.
Courtesy of Howard Folsom

Next four pictures are postcards showing people enjoying the beaches at Corona del Mar.

Courtesy of the Sherman Library

CORONA DEL MAR OVERLOOKING ENTRANCE TO NEWPORT HARBOR, CALIFORNIA—47

Homes built on the top of the cliffs.
Courtesy of the Sherman Library

Goldenrod Footbridge in the 1950s.
Courtesy of Howard Folsom

Artist Joan Irving of the
footbridge in late 1960s.

Goldenrod Footbridge in the 1960s.
Courtesy of Howard Folsom

Promotion at the Port Theater - 1952.
Courtesy of Howard Folsom

Corona del Mar Post Office — de-capitalizing the 'd' in del. This program affected other communities in Orange County as well. The present Post Office in Corona del Mar opened in 1952.

People started buying lots and Corona del Mar expanded to it's seams. Houses that had been there since 1910 were being replaced by newer structures and by 1950, most lots were built out. There was just no room for more. George Hart's dream had taken nearly a half a century to be fulfilled, yet the dream was not over, expansion was on the way.

The nautical themed Port Theater, opened in 1950 and played Cecil B Demille's *Greatest Show on Earth,* with a live elephant out front. Seating 550 plus 350 in the balcony, the Port ran first run movies, then art films.

Significantly, the Sherman Foundation was established in 1951. This would lead to the opening of the Sherman Library and Gardens by Arnold D. Haskel, within just a few years. Haskel started the Library and Gardens for his mentor and

Aerial view of Corona Highlands under construction.
Courtesy of Howard Folsom

benefactor Sherman.

M. H. Sherman had began an electric railway in Los Angeles in the 1890s. This was later acquired by Huntington to become part of the vast Pacific Electric Railway. Ironically, the Pacific Electric had been promised to reach the budding community of Corona del Mar, stopped short in Balboa.

Shore Cliffs was the first development to be established outside the Village. It began in 1951 with the area southwest of the Coast Highway, just on the other side of Buck Gully. This had been Irvine ranch land. Land that was never sold to Hart or his contemporaries. This was the area where children had played and gathered mushrooms. Where cattle had roamed on the bluffs and where stray bulls, suddenly made the open range no-man's-land. Now it was any man's land, for the right price: an ocean view lot could go for $15,000.

The new development was so popular, the northeast area of Shore Cliffs, opened in 1952. Also within Newport Beach,

Coast Highway in the 50s, Ragans, Crown Hardware, & Hampton's Drugs.
Courtesy of Howard Folsom

Miss Muffet Shoppe at Goldenrod in the 1960s.
Courtesy of Howard Folsom

Coast Highway looking north in 1950s.
Courtesy of Howard Folsom

Aerial of Boy Scout Jamboree in 1953.
Courtesy of Howard Folsom

Announcing the Lobster Bake.
Courtesy of Howard Folsom

Two scouts looking out over
Little Corona.
Courtesy of Howard Folsom

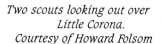

this meant the city was expanding and services would be needed. Schools, parks, and supporting departments like fire and police would be in demand.

Inspiration Point, long a favored vista in Corona del Mar, was offered up in the sale of four lots in 1952. Charles Adams and his wife, proposed the sale — only if a park were established for public use. In addition, they promised $27,000 toward the project, such that a committee was set up by Lester Jones, and donations were sought. A $1.00 per-square-foot donation fund was established toward the park's preservation.

A year later, the Harbor View Elementary School opened for grades Kindergarten through the 5th grade, and could hold 560 students. Also the Corona del Mar Youth Center was set up by Grant Howard during 1954. The Coast Highway was widened in 1955, from 40 feet to 76, including curbs.

The Boy Scout Jamboree in 1953, brought thousands of boys to Corona del Mar. Camping on the hills above the little community, boys from all over the world, enjoyed the open countryside by the sea. Jamboree road as well, became a fixture of the community, having been built expressly for the Scouting event.

Also in the 1950s, many businesses got their start. The Snack Shop opened on Coast Highway. John McIntosh operated the cafe and cooked, while his wife Audrey was the waitress. Later this became a Coco's and then Ruby's. The True Value Hardware store started up with a toy store sharing the right half of the building.

Dennie's Cafe, owned by Mrs. Dennison, started as well. Utility bills could be paid here and the Greyhound Bus Station was next door. Hemingway's

The Snack Shop crew.
Courtesy of Howard Folsom

Iris

Iris means rainbow in Greek and Garden irises come in a broad spectrum of colors. Cut flower irises are mostly blue, white and yellow, while other colors can be navy, blue, white, yellow and combinations. Irises belong to the family of Iridaceae, including freesias. Most spring flowers are related to each other, and grow from bulbs or other forms of underground root stocks (rhizomes.)

restaurant was a satellite of the famous Balboa Hemingway's. Ragan's too, was a prominent restaurant in Corona del Mar. "Cap" Ragan was the owner and served lunch and dinner. Dances were held as well as an 'open mike' night on Fridays, where customers were allowed to show off.

Hampton's Pharmacy also began in the '50s when Mr. Hampton operated the original pharmacy. La Cantina too, began by 1950, next to a dry cleaners. Franklin Realty opened next door in 1953.

Anthony's Shoe Repair, an early business, won many awards for their work, but notably was the repair shop for The Irvine Ranch hands who came in with their horses. The Coast Barber Shop opened then too, but since the 1960s, Fast Eddie has cut the hair of locals as well as the famous.

West of the Village, Promontory Point began opening in 1955, with Irvine Terrace and Bayside in 1956. These developments

The flood of 1952 at Iris Avenue.
Courtesy of Howard Folsom

The Jamaican Inn.
Courtesy of the Sherman Library

Motel Del Mar.
Courtesy of the
Sherman Library

Irvine Terrace opened in 1956.
Courtesy of Howard Folsom

were built on the 360 acres of open lands from George Hart's original land purchase, sold by The Irvine Company back in 1904 — and returned in 1906. Corona del Mar was now perhaps, all of 1,000 acres; larger than Hart even could have imagined.

The Kirkwood Motel.
Courtesy of the Sherman Library

People were coming to the beach for recreation and Corona del Mar responded. The Jamaican Inn was built in 1956 on the Coast Highway at Avocado, the first construction in the area

Sailing regatta off of Corona del Mar.
Courtesy of Howard Folsom

Overview of The Channel Reef Condominiums.
Courtesy of the Sherman Library

Sunset photo of the jetties at Corona del Mar.
Courtesy of the Sherman Library

Coast Highway in the 1960s.
Courtesy of the Sherman Library

Big Corona Beach.
Courtesy of the Sherman Library

just west of the Village. Then followed the Kirkwood Motel at the east end of the Village, and the Del Mar Motel. The Channel Reef Condominiums, boasted a club and penthouse, sat next to the Kerckhoff Marine Lab. All three of these hostels are now gone.

Below is a sketch of the Sherman Library and Gardens.
Courtesy of the Sherman Library

Seven photos of Sherman
Gardens.
Courtesy ofthe Sherman
Library

The Sherman Library and Gardens opened in 1966, adjacent to the original Corona del Mar Elementary School. The new development Cameo Shores started up in 1959, south of Shore Cliffs, and Cameo Highlands, across the highway, came the following year. The public Library too, moved to its present location, with a new building constructed at a cost of $29,000.

Postcards of Corona del Mar.
Courtesy of the Sherman Library

Most significant during the 1960s, was the opening of the Five Crowns at the old Hurley Bell, begun as a private home in 1939. Later renovated and restored as a restaurant, it came into it's own when the owners of Lawry's Restaurants in Los Angeles, took over.

While it has prominent buildings and scenic vistas within it's borders, the best way to see Corona del Mar is from the air. The following photographs taken from the 1920s to the present day, show the historic growth of the community, and provide the feeling of it's majestic vistas.

The Einora Anchor

"In the 1970s, an anchor was found near the Newport harbor entrance, close to the Irvine Pool House. Classed as an admiralty style anchor, it would have been a primary anchor of the schooner class ships, used in the late 1800s along the California coast. It was placed on display in front of the Newport Harbor Patrol as a California State Marine Antiquity, the anchor weighed in at over 1,000 lbs. and measured six feet across and seven feet tall.

"A recent rebuilding of the harbor patrol allowed the removal of the anchor and the orchestration of it's placement off the coast of Crystal Cove State Park. The anchor is now located 150 yards offshore in 20 feet of water and is used as a recreational dive site for scuba and skin divers. The location is out from the Muddy Creek landing, south of Reef Point. The anchor site is also to be used for underwater archeological research in locating and mapping exercises."

Ken Kramer, Crystal Cove State Park

Between the jetties at Corona del Mar.

Courtesy of the Sherman Library

CHAPTER 7
Above Corona del Mar

*K*nowing that aviation began on the west coast in 1910, it is not surprising that aerial photography began shortly thereafter. The first flight from the waters of Newport Harbor, occured in 1912, when Glen Martin flew his bi-plane to Santa Catalina Island and back. The following sequence of aerial photos — many from local photographers — perhaps best shows off the Village and the growth it achieved as a part of Newport Beach over the last century.

A panorama of the harbor, showing a regatta of boats.

1926 The harbor entrance and the west jetty, showing the few existing homes in the Village.   Courtesy of the Sherman Library

1927 A view of the bay, giving a look at the sand bars within the harbor, and a look at the new east jetty.   Courtesy of the Sherman Library

1928 With a better view of the Village, the newly graded streets can be easily seen.   *Courtesy of the Sherman Library*

1929 Trees line the streets of Corona del Mar, while the harbor is shown clear of the sand bars.   *Courtesy of the Sherman Library*

1930 This Village overview, shows Big Corona, Little Corona, and Pacific Gulch. *Courtesy of the Sherman Library*

1931 A panorama of sea, bluffs, and highlands over Corona del Mar. *Courtesy of the Sherman Library*

1932 The harbor entrance sand bar has returned in this view.
Courtesy of the Sherman Library

1946 Aerial photos are absent from the early 1930s, until the late 1940s
because of the depression and WWII.   *Courtesy of the US Navy*

1947-1949 This sequence of the Village, shows the great buildup after WWII and the addition of MacArthur Blvd. Courtesy of the Sherman Library

1948 The sequence of the Village.
Courtesy of the Sherman Library

1949 The sequence of the Village.
Courtesy of the Sherman Library

1951 A classic coastal shot, showing the isolation of the Village.
Courtesy of the Sherman Library

1952 Showing the construction of Shore Cliffs.
Courtesy of the Sherman Library

1953 Majestic view of Newport Beach.
Courtesy of Howard Folsom

1953 The Boy Scout Jamboree.
Courtesy of the Sherman Library

1953 The Boy Scout Jamboree.
Courtesy of Howard Folsom

1954 A high altitude view of Newport Beach.
Courtesy of the Sherman Library

1955 Gives a view of Jamboree road and the bridge to Balboa Island and the development of Bayside.   *Courtesy of the Sherman Library*

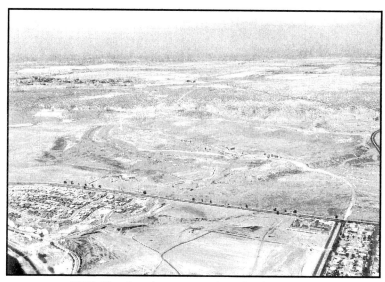

1956 Showing the construction of Irvine Terrace.
Courtesy of the Sherman Library

1957 Looking down on the newly completed Jamaican Inn at Avocado and
Coast Highway. *Courtesy of the Sherman Library*

1958 Showing MacArthur Blvd, Coast Highway, and Irvine Terrace.
Courtesy of the Sherman Library

1959 The new development of Cameo Shores is shown with a few homes.
Courtesy of the Sherman Library

1960 Cameo Highlands can be seen in it's early stages in this high view of Newport Beach. *Courtesy of the Sherman Library*

1961 Newport Harbor and Back Bay.
Courtesy of the Sherman Library

1962 Newport Dunes.
Courtesy of the Howard Folsom

1963 Buck Gully.
Courtesy of Howard Folsom

Above Corona del Mar

1966 Shows the startup of Newport Center.
Courtesy of the Sherman Library

1967 A harbor view of MacArthur and Coast Highway.
Courtesy of the Sherman Library

APPENDICES

Brochure from 1937

Index

Colophon

A panorama of the harbor, from up on Corona del Mar, 1920

BROCHURE

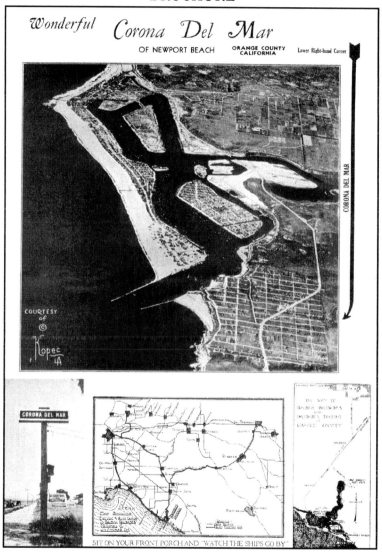

Wonderful *Corona Del Mar*

OF NEWPORT BEACH   ORANGE COUNTY
CALIFORNIA   Lower Right-hand Corner

CORONA DEL MAR

COURTESY of

CORONA DEL MAR

SIT ON YOUR FRONT PORCH AND "WATCH THE SHIPS GO BY"

153

TO PROSPECTIVE PURCHASERS

OF BEACH REAL ESTATE

"WE SAY"

EVERY RIGHT-MINDED MAN AND WOMAN SHOULD PROVIDE FOR THE FUTURE HEALTH AND WELFARE OF THEMSELVES AND THOSE DEPENDENT UPON THEM . . . WHAT IS BETTER THAN A BEACH HOME? . . WHAT OFFERS MORE ADVANTAGES? . . . THINK OF LONG NIGHTS OF PEACEFUL AND RESTFUL SLEEP AFTER DAYS OF BREATHING THE PURE SALT AIR, BASKING ON THE SAND IN THE SUN'S RAYS, SWIMMING IN THE INVIGORATING SALT WATER, FISHING, BOATING, AND OTHER AQUATIC SPORTS, WHICH NOT ONLY MAKE LIFE WORTH LIVING BUT ALSO BUILD HEALTHY BODIES AND MINDS, MAKING FOR A LONGER AND HAPPIER LIFE.

PLEASE DON'T THINK THIS IS SELFISH ADVICE . . . THINK AGAIN . . . IT IS A FORMULA WHICH HAS BEEN "TRIED OUT" AND PROVED "OUTSTANDINGLY" SUCCESSFUL.

OUR PROPERTIES CONSIST OF SAND LOTS—BLUFF LOTS— LEVEL "PALISADES" LOTS A BLOCK FROM THE OCEAN—BLUFF ESTATES FRONTING THE OCEAN—BAY PARCELS, SOME WITH BOAT ANCHORAGE—WHICH FROM THE STANDPOINT OF YOUR OWN EDUCATION, SHOULD BE JUST CAUSE FOR YOUR ASKING OUR TRACT SALESMAN TO SHOW YOU OVER OUR *CORONA DEL MAR* PROPERTIES.

REMEMBER . . . NO SHACKS, NOR THE USUAL BEACH HORRORS SUCH AS MAY BE SEEN ALONG THE COAST IN MANY PLACES, MARRING AND DESTROYING WHAT MIGHT HAVE BEEN A BEAUTIFUL COMMUNITY . . . NO-SIR-EE . . . OUR PROPERTIES ARE RESTRICTED AGAINST SUCH "BEACH HORRORS."

Corona Del Mar

Newport Beach

Magnificent
in the Nobility
of Its Setting

Admirable
in the Charm
and Refinement of
Its Appointments

Dazzling
in the Hospitality
of a Mediterranean
Atmosphere

Matchless
as a Recreation
Rendezvous

A Most Distinguished
Setting for People
Seeking "the Most
Unusual and Delightful"
Location for
a Beach Home

Where Climate, Scenery,
Swimming, Yachting, Etc.
are Important Factors
to be Considered

Newport Bay
Is a Wonderful
Natural Harbor —

The Only Natural Harbor
Between San Diego
and Santa Barbara

LIVE WHERE LIVING IS WORTH WHILE

RECREATIONS

Go direct to our Main Tract Office and ask
MR. S. W. WHITCHER
for information desired, or write, phone
or call on
JOHN SHERROD HARRIS

Numerous and Diversified
Yachts Make Their
Moorings Here

The Flow of
Newcomers, Especially
Owners of Pleasure Craft

And Lovers of Aquatic Sports,
Is Becoming Greater
Each Year

Balboa Yacht Club
Newport Harbor Yacht Club
and Yacht Basins Close By

In Addition to the Adult
Yachting and Sailing Clubs
there are Junior Organizations
for Boys and Girls

Who are Trained in the Various
Aquatic Sports and in
Practical Seamanship

Newport Beach
Is Growing Rapidly

The Community Life
Is Well Worth Considering
when One Is Buying
A Beach Home

UNIT ONE

Let us show you these beautiful
SAND LOTS and
BLUFF LOTS

Diversified Shapes, Sizes and Prices.

Nothing on Pacific Coast Like Them.

Ask "Our" Tract Salesman
Phone Newport Beach 560

SAND SITES—extending from County Road to Waters of the Bay.

BLUFF SITES — fronting on Carnation Avenue, with unobstructed and unsurpassed view.

OUR SALESMEN ARE GENTLEMEN—NO "HIGH-PRESSURE" METHODS USED

What This Harbor Looked Like Some Years Ago

What Our "Unit One" Looked Like Two Years Ago

UNIT ONE

*The White Spot
of the Pacific Coast
for a Beach Home*

CONSIDER THE GROWTH
OF CORONA DEL MAR
DURING THE PAST
THREE YEARS

IF THE SAME GROWTH
DURING THE NEXT
THREE YEARS,
SHOULDN'T VALUES
INCREASE?

Such "Moving Pictures" with Constantly Changing Scenes Free to Residents or Visitors in Corona Del Mar

View of One Portion of "Unit One" Today
Using the past development as a guide, no doubt this view will greatly change in the near future. Purchase your homesite now from the owners while the prices are low and terms are extremely easy.

LET US SHOW YOU
OUR BEAUTIFUL
BLUFF HOMESITES

A GENERAL VIEW OF A

These lots have frontage on Ocean Boulevard and run through to Breakers Drive—see street in center picture showing enclosed subdivision. The house shown below is built on one of these sites.

REALLY A "CREATION"

It is worth your time to go through this model "bluff-beach" home. The view of ocean and bay—even Catalina Island at times—can never be obstructed.

SEE IT

Residence, Residential-Income and Business Lots—at price

ANOTHER GENERAL VIEW OF

ANOTHER VIEW OF OUR BLUFF SITES

Take "time out" and let our Salesmen show you these sites and explain to you the many, many advantages, the restrictions, etc.

PRICES AND TERMS YOU'LL LIKE

PORTION OF UNIT THREE

...nd terms which should interest any "beach-minded" person

A PORTION OF UNIT THREE

SEE THE OCEAN AND BAY

7 BUSINESS LOTS
next to the business building shown in center picture.
ASK FOR PRICE AND TERMS

ANOTHER OCEAN AND BAY VIEW

RESIDENTIAL INCOME LOTS for double bunga-
low court or apartment. Let us show you this IDEAL
SPOT

RESIDENCE SITE—ON THE SAND
Close to Ocean—and at a price of $850, even "Old
Man Grumpy" should buy it as a homesite or an in-
vestment.

OUR TRACT SALES STATION FOR
UNIT THREE
At the foot of the ramp, at the entrance to the enclosed
subdivision

UNIT TWO

MOST OF OUR UNSOLD LOTS IN THIS UNIT ARE FOR SALE IN PAIRS—
MEANING THAT EACH BUILDING SITE FRONTS ON 2 STREETS, PER-
MITTING EACH HOME ON A PAIR OF LOTS TO HAVE ITS OWN PRIVATE
ENCLOSED SAND BEACH.

THEN TOO — WE HAVE A FEW INDIVIDUAL LOTS — VARIOUS SHAPES
AND SIZES, AT PRICES THAT SHOULD INTEREST THE MOST SKEPTICAL.

"OUR"

MAIN

TRACT

OFFICE

"ASK THERE"

"OUR"

MR. WHITCHER
WILL ANSWER
"TRUTHFULLY"
YOUR QUESTIONS

"ASK HIM"

Ask a Tract Salesman to give you a plat of this Unit—or of Units One, Three or Four.
If you like, he will accompany you over all Units, showing you our properties and giving
you full information regarding any parcel. No obligation on your part. Our men are
instructed not to use any methods even bordering on "High Pressure" and we do not
believe they will. If interested in any particular parcel, have the salesman take you
to the Main Tract Office and go over the situation with our Manager, Mr. S. W. Whitcher.

We take pride in doing everything possible to maintain a "high type" of personnel in
our sales organization. We invite constructive criticism and suggestions from the
public as to any change we might make to improve the present high standard of our
CORONA DEL MAR Sales Organization.

WE HAVE FOR SALE IN UNITS ONE
AND TWO:
Sand lots fronting on the bay.
Bluff lots overlooking the bay.
IN UNIT THREE:
Sand lots close to the ocean,
Bluff lots overlooking ocean and bay
IN UNIT FOUR, ABOVE OCEAN BLVD
New houses.
Level lots.

UNIT TWO

OUR
TRACT
SALESMAN

At His Station
"Ask Him"

THIS STATION
Is at Foot of
Ramp as Shown
in Unit Two
"Ask Him"

A View of a Portion of Unit Two

WE SAY—IF YOU ARE GOING TO BUY A BEACH SITE
"BUY SOMEWHERE IN NEWPORT BEACH"

NATURALLY, WE HOPE YOU WILL LOOK OVER OUR PROPERTIES IN

CORONA DEL MAR

BEFORE MAKING YOUR DEFINITE DECISION AS TO WHAT AND WHERE YOU WILL BUY.
WE RECOMMEND THAT YOU CONSIDER CAREFULLY ALL THE ADVANTAGES AND DIS-
ADVANTAGES OF EACH LOCATION—THEN BUY THAT WHICH SUITS YOU BEST.

View of Another Portion of Unit Two

This is an authentic 1937 brochure that was used to sell the original Corona del Mar tracts. It has been carefully
reproduced for your interest and enjoyment by Unique Homes Real Estate. Our phone number really is 875-6000.

UNIT FOUR

PALISADES TAVERN
OPEN
Phone Newport Beach 1416

HOTEL ROOMS

or FURNISHED BUNGALOWS

IN THE COURT

HAVE THE HOSTESS SHOW YOU THROUGH

AND GIVE YOU RATES

CONDUCTED IN A HIGH-CLASS MANNER

THAT WILL BE APPRECIATED

BY THE CLASS OF PEOPLE

WE PREFER TO CATER TO

THIS ENTIRE PROPERTY IS FOR SALE, TOO
Go direct to our Main Tract Office and ask

MR. S. W. WHITCHER
Our Tract Manager, personally, regarding this
particular property, or write, phone, or call on

JOHN SHERROD HARRIS

UNIT FOUR

PALISADES TAVERN
OPEN
Phone Newport Beach 1456

HOTEL ROOMS

or FURNISHED BUNGALOWS

IN THE COURT

HAVE THE HOSTESS SHOW YOU THROUGH

AND GIVE YOU RATES

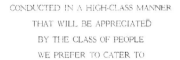

CONDUCTED IN A HIGH-CLASS MANNER

THAT WILL BE APPRECIATED

BY THE CLASS OF PEOPLE

WE PREFER TO CATER TO

THIS ENTIRE PROPERTY IS FOR SALE, TOO
Go direct to our Main Tract Office and ask
MR. S. W. WHITCHER
Our Tract Manager, personally, regarding this
particular property, or write, phone, or call on
JOHN SHERROD HARRIS

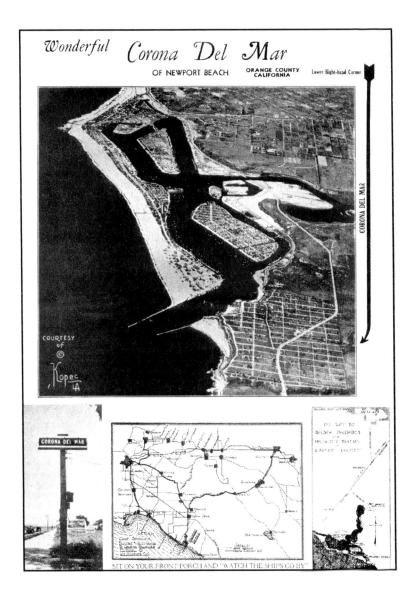

INDEX

A

B

C

N

Newport Beach 16, 18, 23, 24, 67, 68, 70, 79, 86, 119, 135, 142, 144, 147
Newport Dunes 25, 148
Nimmo, Wanda 95

O

Orange 9
Orange County 9

P

Pacific City 24, 29
Pacific Coast Highway 70
Pacific Coast Surf Riding Championships 72
Pacific Electric Railway 23, 33, 41, 48, 51, 119
Pacific Gulch 29, 54, 79, 138
Palisades Hotel 85
Palisades Tavern 53, 63, 72
Paragon 79
Peralta Family 3
Pico, Pio 5, 6, 7
Pier Avenue 25, 29, 33
Poppy 24, 29, 69, 95
Port Theater 118
Promontory Point 25, 124

Q

Quarterdeck 43, 44

R

Rancho Bolsa de San Joaqu´n 3
Rancho Cajon de Santa Ana 10
Rancho Lomas de Santiago 12
Rancho Los Alamitos 10
Rancho Los Cerritos 10
Rancho Los Palos Verdes 10
Rancho San Joaquin 12, 16
Rancho San Justo 10
Red Cars 26, 33, 54
Regidor (Prefect) 3

COLOPHON

This book is set in Caxton, a *Garalde* typeface. Designed by Leslie Usherwood in 1981 for Letraset, it is of an old style design, with a large x-height (small letters.) Having short serifs and high-waisted capitals, it is a text face intended for use in journals and books. The design makes it easy to read in small point sizes.

The typestyle is named for William Caxton, an early printer and the first person to publish in English during 1471, while he was in the Netherlands. He is primarily known for publishing Chaucer's Canterbury Tales in England.

The cover is set in ITC Tiffany is a *transitional* typeface, designed by Ed Benguiat in 1974 for the International Typeface Corporation.

A blend of two typefaces, Tiffany is a combination of Ronaldson, released by MacKellar Smiths & Jordan foundry in 1884, and Caxton, released by the American Type Founders in 1904. The remarkable feature of Tiffany is the exaggerated serifs, used for display work.